Communication for Justice Administration

Theory and Skills

by

HARRY KNIGHT

Golden Gate University

and

WALTER STEVENSON

Golden Gate University

anderson publishing co./cincinnati

Second Printing—August, 1977

ACKNOWLEDGMENTS

Our deep appreciation is due the Pacifica, California, Police Department. Chief Mel Nelson shared extensive technical knowledge with us, as well as pointing the way toward further resources. Captain Charles English arranged for the photograph on the cover.

Material which we used in developing Chapter Seven was gathered in discussions with Ernest Ayala, Director of San Francisco's Centro Latino, and Sergeant Henry Williams of the San Francisco Police Department's Community Relations Unit.

We are indebted to Don Turner and Anne Collins, who at various stages, worked on the manuscript.

Finally, a special thank you is due to Otto Butz, President of Golden Gate University, who helped us begin this project with a Faculty Development Grant, and who encouraged our work all along the way.

CONTENTS

CHAPTER 1

THE COMMUNICATION MODEL

Effective communication is shared thinking. Messages are made of symbols which we present so that others will know what we are thinking. Symbols are elements of expression which represent our thoughts. Words, objects, numbers, and pictures are all examples of symbols.

A symbol can work in many ways at the same time. The law enforcement officer's badge is an example of such a symbol. The word "badge" is a symbol of the object. The badge itself is a symbol of the power vested in the officer. The number on the badge is a symbol of the person wearing the badge. The picture of the government seal represents that social institution of which the police officer is an agent.

The meaning which a person assigns to any message containing symbols depends upon past experience, psychological and physiological needs, and intellectual capabilities.

This is what the study of communication is about.

1. How we transmit meaning to others;
2. How we receive meaning from others;
3. What skills and techniques will help us improve on this exchange of meaning.

THE COMMUNICATION PROCESS

The communication model describes the exchange of messages. This model is constructed of five steps:

1. Encoding the message;
2. Transmitting the message;
3. Receiving the message;
4. Decoding the message;
5. Responding to the message (Feedback).

ENCODING

Encoding is the process of bringing specific sensory reactions into focus to deliver a message. In this preparation stage, the communicator organizes his thoughts, chooses words, and considers the appropriate medium to present his message. For example, in encoding, the communicator may decide to use a harsh voice, write his message, or deliver his message in a formal oral presentation. Whether one decides to deliver an annual report or to alert his partner to the sudden danger of an angrily hurled bottle, encoding must take place. It is the first stage of the communication process in which the communicator identifies what he wishes to communicate and formulates the symbols he intends to use.

Example—A School Visit

Officer Rodriguez is going to visit a junior high school to talk about police work. His goals are to create better relations between the police and the community's teenagers and to interest the students in a future law enforcement career. How can he prepare a message that will meet these goals? Should he use student jargon or should he sound as professional as possible? Should he stress the dangers in violating the law or the rewards of enforcing the law? What will be the symbolic effect if he wears his uniform or appears in plain clothes? Should he make his presentation a discussion or a lecture? Officer Rodriguez is encoding.

TRANSMITTING

Encoding is the choosing process—the preliminary stage in the communication model. Transmitting, on the other hand, is the active process of delivering the message. That is, it is the overt act of communication. Choosing a medium to deliver a message and choosing a specific demeanor are decided in the encoding stage. One's choices, however, are externally manifested in the transmission stage. If a speaker fails to present his ideas effectively, regardless of how well organized his thoughts are, he will have failed in the transmission of his message. The actual delivering of his thoughts determines the speaker's success or failure. The audience not only interprets the message—the symbols—but also the manner in which the message is transmitted.

RECEIVING

Receiving is, simply, the audience's reception of the message. A person receives a message through his senses of seeing, hearing, touching, smelling, and tasting. Most of us receive a message through the use of two or more senses. For example, if we are listening to a speech, we not only hear a message, but we see the speaker. The speaker, by his gestures and facial expressions, transmits certain nonverbal messages which we also interpret. This exchange is often an unconscious exchange which, nevertheless, affects our understanding of one another's meaning.

Example—Conflicting Message

Conflicting messages may be received through two or more senses. If someone is telling us not to be afraid, that he is our friend, but he is standing over us brawny and tight-faced, we'll be frustrated because we are not sure what the real message is—do we trust or fear?

DECODING

Decoding is the process of interpreting the speaker's meaning. In the communication process, a message is encoded, transmitted, received by an audience, and interpreted. In the decoding stage, the meaning of the message is to be deciphered. The audience, in decoding a message, reverses the encoding stage. The speaker, in encoding, transposes meaning into symbols; the audience, on the other hand, converts symbols into meaning in the decoding process.

When we receive conflicting messages, the decoding process becomes more complicated. For example, if someone tells us not to be afraid, but we see (receive) that his lower lip is trembling, decoding, on a satisfactory level, is difficult. In addition, we often interpret on an unconscious level. A pointed finger may bring fear to us not because of what the sender had intended but because of a subconscious fear of parental anger. It is impossible to eliminate subconscious decoding reaction. In most cases, however, the more we interpret on a conscious level (the more skill we develop in bringing previously unconscious decoding to a conscious level), the better we will be able to understand and act on the message we have received.

Example—"Try Harder"

Linda's probation officer ended their review by saying that she hoped Linda would "try harder" next week. In encoding her message, the probation officer chose this phrase to mean "I think you are doing well so I assume that further effort can only mean further improvement." Linda, however, interpreted (decoded) the words to mean, "I do not think you are doing well so, unless you try harder, you are going to fail."

RESPONDING AND FEEDBACK

As each element of the message is decoded, we start the process again as we respond. We respond to the message by encoding our ideas and transmitting them. In responding to a message, we provide the speaker with feedback. Feedback is the integrating factor in the communication process. The feedback cues, simultaneous and rapid, provide infinite stimuli for message transactions. In addition, feedback enables the communicator to judge the effect of his delivery. For instance, a listener's wrinkled brow might indicate to the communicator that he is not being understood. When he notices this feedback indicating confusion, he can adjust his message and try again. Often feedback is subtly absorbed into the communication process. For example, a listener's reassuring nod of the head may encourage more confidence in the speaker. The scowl of a traffic patrol officer may cause the citizen to feel guilty without even knowing if he committed an offense. A complex chain of feedback events develops in any communication exchange. The officer, seeing the citizen "looking guilty," may make assumptions about the person's guilt and assume a stance that is aggressive and disturbing to the citizen. The citizen will then feel even more unsure of himself and probably look more guilty. Both parties in the communication exchange build their messages in response to feedback from the other.

Honest and active feedback, either as a transmitter or receiver, produces effective communication. Dealing squarely with obvious feedback and developing an awareness of subtle forms of feedback, e.g. facial expressions or gestures, will increase the strength and confidence of a communicator.

COMMUNICATION IN ACTION

Listen to a conversation going on around you. The five steps of communication occur in waves and intricate patterns. The steps overlap: the simultaneous cycles of communication form a complex matrix which is constantly changing.

Example—Patrol Car Partners

You're talking to your partner and thinking about how you will respond to your partner's last comment (you are encoding). Your partner senses your hesitation (he is receiving a nonverbal message) and begins to decide what he will say (he is encoding). You finally say something (you are transmitting) and your partner hears your words (he is receiving your oral message). He now prepares a message which will respond to your oral message as well as to your nonverbal hesitation. As he begins to reply, you raise your arm defensively (you are transmitting another nonverbal message).

In a communication transaction, not all elements of each message are equally important. The transaction becomes a pattern of message cues. The sender is responsible for emphasis conveyed during the transmission of his message. Misunderstanding enters the exchange when cues are misinterpreted, unconsciously delivered, or transmitted in a confusing manner.

DISTORTION IN THE COMMUNICATION PROCESS

Distortion in Encoding

The encoding process may be distorted by a number of factors. Sorting one's ideas may be hampered by anything from a distracting background noise to a subconscious emotional interference. A person may be so emotionally involved in the content of the message that he may not be able to put it into words. We learn from an early age to avoid using certain taboo words, phrases, and concepts. This may result in conscious semantic manipulation in encoding a message. Conscious semantic manipulation occurs when a communicator purposely uses words which he knows will upset the receiver or which will bring about some other predetermined reaction. A speaker may refer to strikers as "bands of hoodlums" in order to persuade his audience to act against the pickets. Or the speaker might refer to the strikers as "brave vanguards" in order to persuade his audience to support the pickets.

Distortion in Transmitting

An imprecisely pronounced word can distort the transmission of an oral message. An incorrect word is capable of changing the entire meaning of a message. Also, loud noises or voice interference in the medium through which the message is sent will distort what is received. For example, distortion can be as obvious as a lisp, accent, dialect or a lump in the throat.

Distortion in Receiving

The message received also can be distorted by things such as poor hearing, lack of attention, defensive reaction to the tone of the message, poor eyesight, or lack of awareness of the communication process.

Distortion in Decoding

Distortion can take place in the decoding process in many of the same ways that distortion takes place in the encoding process. For example, semantic interpretation of words and ideas can change the message from what it was intended to be. Personal anxieties and fears, psychological and physiological needs, educational level, personal background and interests, and special areas of knowledge are all sources of distortion in the decoding process.

SUMMARY

Although we are using a model to study communication, actual communication is not that simple. In this complex series of transactions we can isolate five steps—encoding, transmitting, receiving, decoding, and responding. In reality, however, they are not isolated steps following a neatly predetermined pattern. Feedback and distortion complicate the model so that it more closely represents reality. But even then we only study these elements as isolated phenomena so that we can understand them better. Sometimes the five-step process is not completed because of distortion.

Discussion Questions

1. Discuss a story (novel, film, play, television show) in which the central theme was distortion in communication.
2. It is often said that no two people can completely communicate their thoughts. At what points in the communication model are problems likely to arise?

Exercises

1. Think of yourself preparing to present a problem to your superior within a law enforcement agency. Briefly describe how you would be likely to transmit.
2. Think of yourself preparing to deal with a particular unruly child. Briefly list considerations you would have in mind while encoding. Briefly describe how you would be likely to transmit.
3. Focus on your own prejudices and emotions. Make a list of those words which are most likely to create distortion in your own decoding. Now do the same for someone with whom you frequently exchange messages.

CHAPTER 2

COMMUNICATION SKILLS— PREPARING THE MESSAGE

Law enforcement officers are continually confronted with situations in which they must communicate. In Chapter 1, we learned that for communication to take place, there must be an interaction of message and feedback. Chapter two describes the five steps involved in preparing the message:

1. Conceiving the needs of both the sender and the receiver;
2. Setting up the message;
3. Selecting the medium;
4. Organizing the message;
5. Choosing language.

In difficult communication situations, we sometimes do not know where to start. Teenagers assail you as a "pig." Your spouse misinterprets your responses to the pressures of your job. Your commanding officer belittles your work. Your auto mechanic has just cheated you on a repair bill.

Where do you start?

STEP ONE: CONCEIVING NEEDS

Begin by deciding the needs of your audience. As a communicator, you also have certain needs which must be met. A good way to start learning to conceive needs is to jot down your needs as a sender, and your audience's, as a receiver. These notes help you sort your thoughts and may help you to define your problem.

Communication Needs Chart

Receiver's Needs	Sender's Needs
Keep goodwill of customer.	Get a refund.
Increase profit.	Keep goodwill of garage owner.
Keep state certification licenses.	Keep car running.
	Indicate distress.
Keep out of trouble with the law.	Get car repaired in time for upcoming trip.
Gain more customers by word of mouth.	
Increase owner's knowledge of preventive maintenance.	

The "Communication Needs Chart" is a note sheet on which to collect your thoughts. The righthand column is for writing down your needs as the sender. For example, if you are having trouble with your auto repairman, one of your needs is to get a refund on an overcharge. Another need might be for you to keep good relations with him because his is the only garage that is convenient. Another need might be for you to indicate that you are upset with his service so that he will give you better service in the future.

Many times, when you are representing a law enforcement agency, one of your most important needs is to have a good image. Push yourself to get all of your needs out on the sheet, no matter how ridiculous they may seem to you at the time. Then go to the other side of the chart. In the lefthand column, list all of the needs your receiver has relating to your communication. You might list things such as keep goodwill of customers; increase profit; keep state certification licenses; keep out of trouble with the law; gain customers by word of mouth; present an image of efficiency and good will; and increase owner's knowledge of preventive maintenance. Keep going until you have exhausted all the possibilities.

You will find that starting with your own (sender) needs helps you perceive some of the receiver's needs. This process will keep your message oriented toward your audience. Notice that some of the receiver's needs are the same as your own.

The needs chart helps you to organize your message. As you look over your needs chart, then, you are ready to set up the message.

STEP TWO: SETTING UP THE MESSAGE

Look over your needs chart to see which items appear on both sides of the list. These are priority items. They are the places to start your message. These items are very likely to be common objectives shared by you and the person who will receive your message.

DECIDING THE OBJECTIVE

On the basis of your needs chart, decide which item you wish to set up as your primary objective. In a letter there probably won't be much more included than this one objective. In a telephone conversation, this objective probably will be what starts off your conversation, although much more than this one objective will be covered.

In a speech, you may have several parallel objectives of equal importance. The speech probably will be longer than the letter, but less interactive than the phone conversation. Just the same, your needs chart should help you determine just what your objective is.

In an interview, the needs chart can help you perceive things from the point of view of the person being interviewed. This insight may change your technique of interviewing, help you anticipate some questions that you haven't thought of before, cause you to be better prepared, or help you be less defensive or less obnoxious. In preparing for interrogation, the needs chart can help you organize your line of attack and anticipate the defense you are likely to encounter.

Whatever the setting you are communicating in, using the needs chart beforehand to analyze your own needs as a sender, and to recognize the needs of the receiver, will help you plan a better message strategy.

DIFFERENTIATING FACTS, OPINIONS, AND ASSUMPTIONS

Once you have conceived your needs and the needs of your

audience, you are ready to decide the basis for presenting the message. In preparing your message, it is necessary to differentiate between statements of fact, statements of assumption, and statements of opinion. If you do not have a clear idea of the difference between these statements, your message can be criticized as unclear, unreasonable, or illogical.

Facts

Facts may be defined as statements which are verified, not only within our own limited experience, but also within the experience of many others.

In police work, you will be provided with a definition of a "fact" which will evolve from the working relationship of your department and your district attorney's office. In other areas, you must do a little searching for real facts. You might even want to use another needs chart, or continue the one you've already started. List the facts that are known to you as the sender, and then list the facts that are known to the receiver.

Lay them out so you can see them. Look for the holes, and then do the research necessary to fill the gaps. Be sure that you have an adequate definition of a "fact."

Opinions

Opinions may be defined as closely held beliefs of which we are aware but have not verified beyond our own limited experience.

To distinguish opinion from fact is hard at times. Many times we hold opinions so strongly, that we insist they really are facts. This is a shortcoming because we are not ready to tolerate or understand the opinions of those with whom we want to communicate. This biased perspective will create trouble in communicating. We must recognize our opinions as opinions, and not get them confused with facts.

Assumptions

Assumptions may be defined as statements which proceed from opinions and beliefs of which we are unaware and which we therefore do not question. Prejudices are based on assumptions.

Assumptions aren't always easy to spot. It is sometimes helpful to get someone to work with you and listen to the way you are setting the problem up. Ask for feedback from them. Ask them to listen for assumptions that you are making without realizing it. For example, you may dislike another officer because he is lazy and uncooperative. Be sure that what you are taking as fact is not just an assumption on your part. If you were going to set up an interview with this officer to discuss his job performance, it would certainly bias the outcome of the interview if you began already believing that it was a fact that he was lazy. The ability to differentiate statements which contain facts, opinions and assumptions, to recognize them for what they are, is crucial to developing an articulate style of communication.

STEP THREE: SELECTING THE MEDIUM

So far we have discussed the theory of communicating, keeping in mind the role the audience plays as a communicator prepares a message. The "Communication Needs Chart" has been discussed as a device for helping to organize thoughts and feelings into the sender's and the receiver's needs. This technique, theoretically, allows time for developing a full picture of the situation, of identifying priority objectives.

At this point, we are ready to decide possible choice of medium. In some cases, a letter may be sent; in some cases an immediate phone call may be necessary. Other situations may require your setting up a community relations program involving speeches and personal appearances over a period of a few months.

We are also ready to think about some of the alternative ways of expressing our message. For example, if we decide that the medium we will use is television, we certainly would want to take full advantage of the visual image and its impact on communication effectiveness.

STEP FOUR: ORGANIZING THE MESSAGE

After conceiving the needs of both you and your audience, after setting up the problem with primary objectives, after sorting out the facts, the assumptions, the opinions and the alternatives, you are ready to organize the message.

There are many ways of organizing a message. Much depends on who your audience is and what subject matter has priority. It might be helpful to look at some graphic representations of organization.

NARRATE

Tell the story as it happens. Put little emphasis on single points. Maintain a constant pace. Paragraphs emerge out of logical breaking points in the action. For example, hours in the day, days in the week, sketches of different people, or rooms in a building might be logical units into which you divide your narration.

Example of Narration

I was driving through the parking lot of Martin Luther King High School when I saw the two suspects climbing over the fence. I pulled my car over next to the fence just as they landed on the blacktop. I ordered them to stop and they did so. They were each carrying a canvas bag containing sporting goods marked as property of the school.

The next afternoon, I was approached by the attorney representing one of the suspects and told by him that I was accused of assaulting his client. I immediately reported this to my captain.

AMPLIFY

Make your statement clearly and precisely. Continue by elaborating and expanding on what you originally said. As you move from thought unit to thought unit, your original statement is amplified so that the picture you are describing becomes clearer to your audience. Paragraphs emerge as a result of your movement from unit to unit of your original statement.

Example of Amplification

Television cameras are beginning to appear in today's courtrooms. Television gives the public a clearer understanding of courtroom procedure. Television makes our justice system real for our citizens.

Introducing television into the courtroom is an example of how modern justice administration is using technology to improve its efficiency and to educate the public.

DEVELOP

State your position. Each part of your argument will be a subsection of your report. Develop each of these subsections by example. (You may also want to use one of the other methods of organization for developing each of the subsections.) Paragraphs emerge from each of your carefully thought out examples.

Example of Development

As societies go through the three basic stages of economic development, men allocate their work energy in different ways.

The first stage is the agrarian. In this stage, men direct all their work to growing their food. Examples of these workers are farmers and shepherds.

The second stage is industrial. In this stage, men direct all their work to manufacturing. Examples of these workers are weavers and miners.

The third stage is service. In this stage, men direct all their work to meeting non-material needs. Examples are teachers and police officers.

PRO CON

State your position (decision, recommendation, argument). Then move from issue to issue stating the pro and then the con argument for each issue. Each issue is the subject matter for a new paragraph.

Example of Pro-Con (Debate)

As warden, I am compelled to confine all inmates for the next twelve hours. This has not been an easy decision.

On the one hand, I have been urged not to do this because of what it might do to the institution's public image. But on the other hand, confinement will prevent any further acts of violence.

Confinement may lower the morale of the inmates, but it will also give everyone a cooling off period.

Confinement may not solve all the problems of this institution, but I am responsible for the safety of all persons here, both inmates and employees.

DEFEND

State your position. Then tell why your statement is true. You will explain and defend through a series of precisely expressed parallel statements. Paragraphs emerge from each area of defense.

Example of Defense

Probation officers should receive training in self-defense.

This is because of the physical dangers inherent in their work.

The present program is inadequate because this training is lacking.

Our probation officers will be more confident in their work as a result of this training.

JUSTIFY

Make a recommendation (it could be expressed as a statement.) Then relate the facts that support this statement and make it a logical decision. Much justification uses financial data as documentation. Paragraphs emerge from each of the facts you present.

Example of Justification

Promotion of Officer Tuan is justified by the following.
1. His service record is outstanding.
2. He ranked first on the examination.
3. He has been with the department longer than any other candidate.

ARGUE

State your position. Then state a major objection to your position. Logically defeat this argument. Then go on to the next argument against your statement and logically defeat this objection. New paragraphs are formed each time you switch from argument to argument.

Example of Argument

This department should move to staggered shifts. One major objection to this has been that staggered shifts disrupt home life. However, staggered shifts would give every officer equal access to completely free days and completely free evenings.

Another objection has been that staggered shifts will lower morale by removing competition for preferred hours. However, the more democratic distribution pattern of staggered shifts may just as well raise morale.

Whichever organizational structure you choose, it should be easy for your audience to follow. Keep similar kinds of ideas in the same paragraph or section, so that each section builds on what has gone before. Move the sections around until they make sense, and the direction of your message is clear.

STEP FIVE: CHOOSING LANGUAGE

Be sure to use language that can be understood by your audience. The level of language will, of course, vary depending on who your audience is.

It is a mistake to use elementary level language if your reader can understand a more advanced level: this can be insulting, and the insult can work in reverse. Insults will block reception of your message.

You can test your language level by trying it on someone else. For example, if you are writing a letter, let someone else read it, and see what he thinks. Are your words too sophisticated? Are they too simple? If you are going to deliver a speech, have someone else listen to a preview. Find out if he thinks you are talking over his head. If that is the case, your language is probably too sophisticated. Ask for feedback from him. Is the concept too simply stated? Then your level of language is probably too elementary. You might even want to try to listen to or watch yourself using an audiotape recorder or a videotape recorder. In the case of a letter, set it aside for a while, and then go back to it and reread it. Ask those same questions. Is the tone condescending? Will the reader feel that it is an adult talking to another adult?

TECHNICAL JARGON

Eliminate unnecessary technical jargon when you are developing your message and choosing language. What seems obvious to you as the sender may be terribly confusing to the receiver. Law enforcement agencies use many abbreviations. There is nothing more confusing than receiving a message in abbreviation code.

Another confusing type of jargon is specialized scientific or professional jargon. For example, if a doctor is trying to describe your illness to you, you understand it best if he uses language that you understand: words like "elbow," "knee cap," "pain," and "heartbeat."

There are two ways to overcome the barrier of technical language. One is to substitute ordinary words for the technical word. Sometimes this is impossible, because there is no simple word that means the same thing. So when you must use a technical word, set up a similar case in ordinary terms or symbols that you know your audience understands. For example, a doctor, in explaining blood flow in the aorta and its relationship to the capillaries, may want to use the stem and leaf structure of a plant as an analogy. This way, the patient can understand what is going on in his own body. If the doctor continues to use his medical language (pulminary, visceral, aortal, pathologic, neuratoxin) his patient will not receive the complete message.

Choosing language is an important part of developing the message. Choose the appropriate level on the particular audience being addressed. Avoid confusing language.

SUMMARY

The five steps involved in preparing the message help the communicator find a place to start. They are essentially involved in the encoding process. These steps focus the attention of the communicator who is encoding on the needs of himself and others, on the thinking from which his ideas will proceed, on the format that will best serve his needs, on the various possibilities of organization, and on the kinds of words he will use.

Discussion Questions

1. The communication model has five basic steps; there are five basic steps in preparing the message. What similarities do you see between these two sets of steps?
2. Discuss policing situations in which problems are created by the failure to differentiate between facts, assumptions and opinions.
3. You are the supervising officer for an investigative team, one member of which has just been killed in the line of duty. It is your responsibility to inform the family. They live in a distant city. Would you write a letter, send a telegram, make a phone call, or go to see them in person? Formulate an argument supporting the use of each of these. Then criticize the use of each.

Exercises

1. On a sheet of paper, draw two columns. In one, list all the reasons you can think of for considering the needs of others in preparing a message. In the other, list all the reasons you can think of for considering your own needs in preparing a message. When the two lists are completed, draw lines between columns connecting entries which are essentially the same.

2. Rewrite two of the seven examples of organizing the message using at least three of the other ways of organizing.

3. Make a list of the jargon in your office. Expand that list to include particular jargon in your organization. Make a third list which expands the other two and which includes jargon unique to your field or profession.

4. Take the above lists, and for each term, write alternative ways of saying what each term means.

5. Prepare a brief message dealing with some aspect of the general topic of higher education programs for law enforcement officers. Use all five steps in preparing your message. Present it to your class for criticism.

CHAPTER 3

NONVERBAL COMMUNICATION

Oral communication is primarily a process of exchanging words. However, this chapter will discuss the important role of the gestures and movements which accompany the exchange of words. In addition, we will discuss the role of objects in transmitting messages nonverbally.

Nonverbal communication is communication which does not rely on either spoken or written words. More specifically, nonverbals are body and face movements ("kinetic configurations") which humans use to accentuate, articulate, and amplify oral messages or objects which humans arrange for conscious or unconscious statements.

NONVERBAL CONTEXT

Nonverbal communication, like other kinds of transmissions gains much of its meaning from context. It is difficult to read a person like a book by observing folded arms, crossed legs, or a wrinkled brow. Although there are certain universal nonverbal signs, context verifies meaning.

Example: Context (Kinetic Configuration)

While officer Gomez drives, his partner sits sideways in his seat, talking. He holds a cup of coffee between them and never puts it down.

Officer Gomez may know from a "body language" book that this gesture is one of closed, exclusive feelings. It is a distancing mechanism.

However, an examination of the context reveals that there is no place in the moving patrol car to safely set the coffee. To place it anywhere other than in his hands would be to risk spilling it.

Example—Context (Material Objects)

When Inspector Chung was moved into his new office,

he was distressed to see that his desk was placed against a blank wall, while the desks of the other two inspectors were against a large window. He thought that he was being given the least desirable location. When he questioned his superior about this, however, his superior recalled Chung's many complaints about the excessive heat in his former office. Special effort had been made to give him his present location so that he would be directly under the air-conditioning vent.

The context of a nonverbal interchange is much more broadly based than that of a spoken or written interchange. There are a great many factors influencing the context of meaning for nonverbals. Some of these factors contributing to the context of nonverbal communication are:

physical environment (objects, smells, noises, colors, shapes);

emotional environment (anger, nervousness, fear, confidence);

symbolic environment (traditions, norms, mores, philosophies);

sensory environment (taste, touch, smell, sight, hearing).

In a message transmission, these factors influencing context are not always easily distinguished. They are, in fact, not mutually exclusive categories. Rather, they are sets of influences working at once, contributing to the complexity of the message transmission. In trying to decode a message you must be aware of this complexity, and avoid premature assessments of the intention of a particular nonverbal.

NONVERBALS—CULTURAL, REGIONAL, CASTE

Another helpful way of looking at nonverbal communication is to notice the differences in context due to cultural, regional, and caste backgrounds of the people communicating. Misreading nonverbals often occurs when the communication interchange involves participants from different cultural backgrounds. One party misreads the other party's nonverbals. He assumes, incorrectly, that these gestures are intended to have the same meaning they do in his own culture.

Example: Cultural Nonverbals

Americans shake their heads from side to side to signal "no," up and down to signal "yes."

People from many parts of India shake their heads from side to side to indicate "yes."

This causes considerable confusion for Indians in the United States.

Misreading nonverbal message intentions may also come from differences in regional backgrounds. Even in the same language group, there will be sets of regions with different nonverbals. These differences can often lead to misunderstanding. Regional differences are often firmly set in tradition, passed from generation to generation. In the United States, we can identify regional backgrounds from verbal accents and also from regional nonverbals.

Example: Regional Nonverbals

In regions of the United States where hats are worn, men will touch the brim of the hat to indicate respect. Long after these men leave their hat-wearing region, they will still automatically reach up and touch their foreheads to indicate respect.

The differences in nonverbal sets that come with caste are pervasive. By caste, we mean those nonverbal sets which accompany position and status.

Example: Caste Nonverbals

Factory workers having a beer after their shift may playfully punch one another to communicate fellow-feeling and good will.

Executives meeting for cocktails are more likely to confine their physical contact to handshakes.

There are certain nonverbals characteristic of people in power, people with authority. Police organizations use the uniform to aid nonverbal caste differentiation. In meetings, the gavel may be used to indicate authority. Some families set aside certain chairs in the home for members with power or authority.

It is not always possible to separate the three categories of nonverbals. Their effect on communication interchange must be evaluated on the basis of their interrelation.

CONFIGURATIONS OF AGREEMENT

Nonverbals are best viewed as configurations, as opposed to specific gestures or subsets. Configurations are patterns and interrelationships of nonverbal cues. When involved in a communication interchange, it is best to get a feel for the nonverbal aspects of that message transmission by becoming aware of the configurations occurring. The communicator must continually move out of his own personal system, and look at himself objectively. Attempting this objective view of himself will enlarge his potential for becoming aware of the rest of the configuration in which he is involved. For example, if a person you are interviewing is perspiring, you may conclude that he is extremely nervous. If, however, you are able to view the larger context, and therefore allow more nonverbal messages to enter the configuration, you might discover that the room is too warm.

OBJECTS WHICH HAVE SPECIAL MESSAGES

Some objects which have special meaning are required in certain aspects of law enforcement work. Some objects used every day can transmit special messages when used within the context of law enforcement work.

In Chapter One, we discussed the symbolic functions of the badge. The messages it transmits can be received and decoded as threatening or reassuring depending on how the badge is presented. The uniform has a similar function in transmitting messages. When the uniform is worn the officer wearing it is continually transmitting a message to those who see him by describing his role in the community. Weapons carried in the line of duty almost always transmit threatening messages. They will transmit these messages not only when they actually are being used, but also when they are touched or when they come into view because of a shift in clothing.

Objects used every day can acquire special meaning in law enforcement work. Usually these meanings are threatening. The receiver may decode the handling of these objects as transmitting either the officer's hostility or his physical power. Such objects can include:

briefcase	marked car
sunglasses	motorcycle
cigarettes	gloves
keys	helmet
ticket book	legal documents
folders	pens & pencils
typewriter	

CONTINUITY AND DISCONTINUITY OF NONVERBALS

Once you have mastered the observation of nonverbals by configurations rather than specific movements, you can begin to verify meanings. To verify meaning, check for continuity between the verbal message and the nonverbal message being communicated. Simple discontinuity is evidenced in someone saying, "yes," but accompanying that with a head shaking "no." A more complex configuration discontinuity occurs when someone says that he trusts you, but he demonstrates a set of nonverbals which indicates withdrawal. Discovering discontinuity in nonverbals does not mean that you have caught the person in a lie. It may mean, however, that you are going to need to do more (both verbally and nonverbally) to get this person to trust you. Watching for continuity and discontinuity in a respondent's nonverbal configuration is one type of feedback which can help the communicator adjust his message.

SUMMARY

An understanding of the role of nonverbals in the communication interchange can help you become a more effective communicator. Be cautious not to use your understanding of the role of nonverbals glibly. Be aware that there are many factors which create a context for the interpretation of nonverbal communication. Nonverbals are powerful communicators but the sources of meaning are complex. Use your understanding of nonverbals to give you feedback as to how you are doing as a communicator. The effective communicator understands this complexity, even though he may not be able to identify the source of each of the meanings communicated nonverbally. He respects individual differences and looks for configurations of nonverbals. He sees the message being communicated not only in others' nonverbals, but in his own as well.

Discussion Questions

1. Think about the theory of the cultural and regional context of nonverbals, and apply it to your own family. Have you or your family brought such nonverbals with you to this area? Do you or your family exhibit such nonverbals identifying you as residents of a particular area?

2. Think about the theory of the caste context of nonverbals. What kind of nonverbals identify status and rank within an organization with which you are familiar?

3. Discuss a story (novel, film, play, television show) in which problems are created by the misinterpretation of nonverbals.

Exercises

1. Look through a magazine for photographs which use nonverbals to transmit a message. Label your selections given the context of the magazine. Once the photos are removed from the magazine, are alternative interpretations possible?

2. Visit two establishments in your area which compete for essentially the same business or clientele. List nonverbals which make the two different from one another.

3. With a partner, attempt to communicate with nonverbals only. Can you understand one another? Now try to mislead your partner by using nonverbals which have more than one meaning so that he may misinterpret.

4. Pick a scene from a play. Write instructions for each actor explaining in what ways he might create a configuration of nonverbals for his character.

CHAPTER 4

INTERVIEWING

Law enforcement work often requires gathering information from people about unclear situations. Interviewing techniques can help participants ask questions which bring information into focus, reveal attitudes and values, discover common interests, establish areas for further inquiry. Interviewing techniques can be divided into three basic categories by ways of asking questions. The three most common types of questions are:

1. the direct question
2. the reflective question
3. the non-directive (or open) question

THE DIRECT QUESTION

"What is your name?"
"Do you live in this neighborhood?"
"Do you have a driver's license?"
"Have you ever seen this man before?"

As you can see from the rat-a-tat rhythm of the above sentences, the direct question is abrupt. It quickly asks for specific information. Direct questions can usually be answered "yes" and "no." Short answers with specific data are typical alternatives.

The direct question is specific. Therefore, the answers are highly focused. For example, an answer to the question, "Do you live in this neighborhood?" will be a "yes" or "no" without any guarantee of qualification. The interviewee will usually give the briefest answer possible. Not much more information is given than is asked for when the interview is at the direct questioning stage.

The direct question is not effective in pursuing beliefs, attitudes, and feelings. Because they are so specific, the answers to direct questions can often mislead, misrepresent, or only partially answer what the questioner really asked. Nonetheless, the direct question is

27

an important one; it is very helpful as a starting point for an interview.

We can classify the direct question into three types:

1. yes-no
2. forced alternative
3. direct data

Example—Yes-No Questions

"Is your wife living here?"

"Have you seen her within the last week?"

Example—Forced Alternative Questions

"Did she tell you she was on drugs, or did you find out for yourself?"

"Did your social worker tell you your support had been cut off, or did you get a letter from the county?"

Example—Direct Data Questions

"What are the names of friends she might be staying with?"

"How much money did you give her the last time you saw her?"

Sometimes the direct question is referred to as the "closed" question. This is because the interviewer imposes precise limits on the area of response to be covered by the person answering the question.

THE REFLECTIVE QUESTION

In this question the interviewer passively repeats the exact words or phrases of the interviewee. The interviewer must take care not to add his own value judgments to the response of the interviewee.

For example, the interviewee might have ended a response with the words, ". . .and we've been living in that area for six years." The interviewer, employing the reflective questioning technique, would merely say, "In that area. . .?"

In most cases, the interviewer hopes that the interviewee will respond with clarification, elaborating the original response. In contrast to the direct question, the reflective question does not aggressively dictate the area of response.

THE OPEN QUESTION

Compared with the other two types of questions, the open question offers the greatest freedom for the interviewee. The interviewer who uses this technique is asking for feelings, attitudes, and beliefs. But he asks in such a way that the respondent is not led into an answer. The interviewer does not merely maintain the interview by reflecting or repeating what the interviewee has said. The question is expressed precisely, but the response may go in many directions. For example, the following is a list of phrases which may be used by the interviewer to elicit open responses:

"How do you feel about...?"
"What do you think about...?"
"What would you do if...?"
"Tell me about...."
"If you were Mr. Jones, what would you do if...?"
"What was it about him that you didn't like?"

The interviewer who uses the open question can find out a great deal of information from the interviewee. In encouraging the interviewee to do more talking, the open question helps create a relaxed and trusting environment. Because the open question allows the respondent to talk about a particular subject, the interviewer can usually get more information. He can get information which the direct question might miss. The open question also allows movement into new subject areas with ease. This is something that neither the direct question nor the reflective question can do.

The open question can help create an environment in which the interviewer and the interviewee develop rapport. When trust grows, more information (but not necessarily data) is exchanged. The open question is particularly useful when the interviewer is trying to get more than just the facts. He can delve deeper into the interviewee's feelings, beliefs, emotions, and philosophies. In many cases, open questions lead both the interviewer and the interviewee to a more complete understanding of the problem than either would have comprehended if only direct questions were asked.

Interviews are often helped by varying the types of questions asked. Variety helps the interview flow smoothly and logically. Balancing questioning techniques helps move the interview from question to question. Logically and carefully combining the questioning techniques also yields smooth transition among subject areas, establishing a pattern of questions and answers. These can be used later in the interview as references from which future responses can be drawn or clarified. Again and again, experts in the field of interviewing stress the importance of relaxed (but not disordered) interview settings and feelings. Relaxation, however, does not mean lack of direction. The interviewer is expected to be in control without being authoritarian or insensitive. He must keep the interview moving.

Example—Interview: "Suspended Student"

Situation: Alex Cooper has been suspended from high school.

Interviewer: Mr. Jacobson, the high school counselor.

Interviewees: Mr. and Mrs. Cooper, Alex's parents.

Mr. Cooper: Good morning...are you Mr. Jacobson?

Mr. Jacobson: Yes.

Mr. Cooper: We have this letter here from you, Mr. Jacobson. We're the Coopers and we've come about this letter saying Alex has been suspended, and we're supposed to come and see you or something....

Mr. Jacobson: Yes, well...sit down please.

Mr. Cooper: This is my wife, Mrs. Cooper....

Mr. Jacobson: Pleased to meet you, Mrs. Cooper.

Mr. Cooper: ...and I'm Harvey Cooper.

Mr. Jacobson: Harvey, glad to meet you.

Mr. Jacobson: You mentioned the letter....

Mr. Cooper: Yes, I have it here. Do you want to see it?

Mr. Jacobson: No, that's okay. I have a copy of it.

Harvey, what are your feelings about the letter?

Mrs. Cooper: Well, you sent us the letter, Mr. Jacobson. We assumed that you had a reason for bringing us here.

Mr. Jacobson: Well, oftentimes in situations like this, it's best to talk about how you feel. There are a lot of things we can do, but we want to do it together as a team. I'd like to find out what your feelings are. . . .

Mrs. Cooper: But, Mr. Jacobson, I don't know what it is we're going to do. I mean, why did you ask us here? Has our Alex done something wrong that we don't know about?

Mr. Jacobson: There isn't anything that you don't know about, but there is a specific problem that the school is having.

Mr. Cooper: Problem?

Mr. Jacobson: Well it's a series of problems stemming from Alex's resistance to authority.

Mr. Cooper: Well, that's very true. Alex always does seem to resent being told what to do. But if you give these kids their way, no telling how they'll turn out.

Mrs. Cooper: Harvey, you're always too hard on Alex. Alex is a good boy, just give him time to grow up.

Mr. Jacobson: I think you both are talking about a very common kind of behavior in adolescence. I don't think there is anything to be worried about. Resisting authority is typical behavior for teenagers. Actually, it's a very useful behavior in normal development.

But our problem is that Alex is creating disruptions for the people who work with him every day, and these disruptions could be detrimental to his development.

Mrs. Cooper: His development?

Mr. Jacobson: Well, his grades are not good and the teachers are beginning to label him as a problem. Our concern, as a school, is that he get good grades and learn something. That's our job.

How do you feel about his progress in high school and the overall growth of his knowledge?

Mrs. Cooper: Well, I've always hoped that Alex would go

on to college. But I don't think that his father encourages him enough in that direction.

Mr. Jacobson: How do you feel about that, Mr. Cooper?

Mr. Cooper: Well, Mr. Jacobson, I have a lot of respect for people like you who go to college. But you know, I never did, and I think I've made a good living and been a good provider. And so I think that maybe Alex could do just as well if he didn't go to college. Does he have to go to college?

Mr. Jacobson: No, there's no reason why he has to go to college. But we do have to decide what we're going to do about this suspension.

Mrs. Cooper: Well, they have no right to suspend Alex. They're just picking on him.

Mr. Jacobson: In what ways do you see suspension as picking on Alex?

Mrs. Cooper: Well, they just should have told him not to do it again . . . and called me, and I would have told him that he shouldn't cut classes anymore.

Mr. Jacobson: You mentioned that you were interested in Alex's going on to college. What do you feel would be the best experience for him right now?

Mrs. Cooper: Well, he does have his Uncle Elmer who lives in the same town where the State University is. Maybe if he visited with Elmer, he'd be more interested in going to college after high school.

Mr. Jacobson: How do you feel about that, Mr. Cooper?

Mr. Cooper: Well, that seems all right to me. Can he leave school and go visit his uncle?

Mr. Jacobson: Yes, I think I could arrange that.

Analyzing the Interview

A good way to begin analyzing an interview such as "Suspended Student" is to briefly describe the role each participant plays.

The interviewer, Mr. Jacobson, tries to use non-directive questions to explore the Coopers' feelings. Mr. and Mrs. Cooper use direct and reflective questions in an effort to clarify Mr. Jacobson's purpose in interviewing them.

Having described the roles of each participant, we can now attempt a general statement about the direction of the interview as a whole. At its beginning, Mr. Jacobson wanted to know how Alex's parents felt about his suspension. Mrs. Cooper was anxious to defend her son. Mr. Cooper wished to comply with the official request of the school. At the end of the interview, all three work together to plan Alex's visit to his uncle.

Notice how Mr. Jacobson's first attempt to talk about the Coopers' feelings

"Harvey, what are your feelings about the letter?" (non-directive question)

was undermined by Mrs. Cooper's demand for a specific focus for the interview:

"I mean, why did you ask us here?" (direct question)

"Has our Alex done something wrong we don't know about?" (direct question)

Mr. Cooper's reflective question:

"Problem . . . ?"

forces clarification of Mr. Jacobson's intent, and allows Mr. Cooper to talk about his feelings.

As the Coopers stray from the point of the interview as originally conceived by the interviewer, Mr. Jacobson, he must regain control by focusing on the school's concern for Alex's development. Mrs. Cooper's reflective question:

"His development?"

indicates her willingness to concentrate upon the matter at hand. This allows Mr. Jacobson to return to the use of non-directive questions.

"How do you feel about his progress in high school and the overall growth of his knowledge? (non-directive question)

"How do you feel about that, Mr. Cooper?" (non-directive question)

Mr. Cooper moves the interview away from its point.

"Does he have to go to college?" (direct question)

Mr. Jacobson once again returns the interview to the point of its intent.

"In what ways do you see suspension as picking on Alex?" (non-directive)

"What do you feel would be the best experience for him right now?" (non-directive)

An interview is made up of several different kinds of questions. In this particular interview, the interviewer, Mr. Jacobson, relied on his ability to use non-directive questions for control. Many other interviewers, in a longer interview, would use all three kinds of questions discussed in this chapter.

Notice how, in a good interview, all of the participants have a chance to ask questions. The purpose of the interview is to bring the parties together to focus on a common solution or decision. In this particular interview, Mr. Jacobson's non-directive questions have led the participants toward a mutually agreeable course of action: the visit to Alex's uncle.

INTERROGATION

Interrogation is a special case of interviewing. This section stresses the difference between interviewing and interrogating. As a communicator, you must be able to understand these two ways of questioning.

Most of what has been said about interviewing is *not* true for interrogation. In interrogation, a highly aggressive interviewer dominates. The interviewer is prodded by a need for accelerated data responses; the interview atmosphere is coercive rather than supportive.

Here are some significant differences between interviewing and interrogating.

FIGURE 4
DIFFERENCES BETWEEN INTERVIEWING
AND INTERROGATION

	THE INTERVIEW	THE INTERROGATION
Control of Questioning	Shared between all parties. Participatory.	Completely dominated by the interviewer. One-sided.
Purpose of Questioning	To exchange information beneficial to all parties. Mutually beneficial.	To coerce information from interviewee. Not mutually beneficial.
Type of Question	Direct. Reflective. Open ended.	Direct.
Communication Atmosphere	Relaxation. Trust.	Intensity. Coercion. Pressure.

As a result of these differences, several problems emerge for the interviewer. He must be ready to face the fact that the interviewee may use much of his energy for concealment. Because the interrogation usually consists of one direct question after another, the interviewee may become more and more defensive. Concealing answers is a basic strategy of self-defense.

Another problem faced by the interviewer is that he is expected to aggressively coerce information from the interviewee. He must try to "catch" the interviewee off guard. Therefore, instead of building the interview toward trust, he is more likely to create an atmosphere of deception and suspicion. With this atmosphere permeating the interview, it is hard for the interviewer to get the cooperation of the interviewee. This lack of cooperation makes it more difficult for the interviewer to get the information he is after.

Another problem arises for the interviewer because he must "hit" and "miss" with direct questions. He must ask his questions this way because the interviewee usually doesn't cooperate by giving unsolicited information. The "story" the interviewer gets is often fragmented. The interviewer must work additionally hard to get enough information to put the pieces together.

An interrogator also experiences pressure to get vital information fast. Because this information is often needed in a hurry, the interrogator must work at an accelerated pace. This pressure affects the behavior of the interviewer. He may lose some of his sensitivity to the other kinds of communication cues we have talked about. For example, he might be under such pressure that he loses his awareness of nonverbal messages. Or he might mix his own preconceived notions, prejudices and feelings with the interviewee's to such an extent that he cannot separate them. These distorted interpretations may lead to inadequate representations of what really happened.

SUMMARY

This chapter defined interviewing as a process which can be analyzed in terms of the kinds of questions asked. Three kinds of questions were discussed: (1) direct; (2) reflective; and (3) non-directive. The pursuit of quick information by interrogation was contrasted with interviewing techniques to show the different strategies and methods used by each to achieve their distinct ends.

Discussion Questions

1. Discuss situations in which you have seen interviewing techniques being used. Distinguish between interviewing and interrogation in these situations.
2. Find out about the rules for courtroom testimony. What elements of interviewing and interrogating do you find in these rules?
3. The names given the kinds of questions discussed in this chapter are the authors'. Give each kind of question an alternative name. Justify your choice.

Exercises

1. In "Analyzing the Interview," we talked about the direction taken by the example interview in terms of the position of each participant at the beginning of the interview. We proceeded to analyze the interview on the basis of these statements.

   Below is a different version of each participant's position. Rewrite the interview in terms of these new attitudes.

   Mr. Jacobson hopes the Coopers will transfer their son to another school. Mrs. Cooper is frightened that the school will put Alex in a juvenile hall. Mr. Cooper dislikes schools and anyone who works for one.

2. Interviews within the context of law enforcement work include hiring interviews, disciplinary interviews, promotional reviews, and investigation. In what other circumstances related to law enforcement would the techniques discussed in this chapter be useful?

3. Take five of the questions in the example interview and rewrite them so that they become another kind of question.

CHAPTER 5

GIVING ORDERS

Differences Between Interviewing and Giving Orders

	Interviewing	Giving Orders
What type of transmission is used?	Interrogatives (Questions)	Imperatives (Orders)
Who is responsible for the message?	Shared by alternating sender and receiver	sender and receiver
What is the style of control?	Democratic	Authoritarian
What kind of time is needed?	Extended	Brief
How are goals formulated?	Developed during transmission	Served by transmission
How apparent is feedback?	Visible with each transmission	Not built in; must be sought
What is the role of feedback?	Constructing	Clarifying

WHAT TYPE OF TRANSMISSION IS USED?

Interviews are built on sequences of interrogatives; orders exist as independent imperatives. The interrogative is a sentence which asks a question; the imperative is a sentence which gives an order.

Example—Interrogatives and Imperatives

Interrogative	Imperative
"Could you be at Central station in ten minutes?"	"Proceed to Central station immediately."
"How would you describe the damage to Vehicle #2?"	"Describe the damage to Vehicle #2."
"Can our unit help this family?"	"Assign staff to assist this family."

Ironically, orders are sometimes structured as interrogatives. This can be confusing.

Example—Confusing Interrogatives With Imperatives

Interrogative: "Do you know what time it is?"

Imperative: "Please tell me the time."

Interrogative used in place of an imperative: "Can you tell me the time?"

The first sentence in the example clearly asks a question; the second sentence clearly gives a polite order. The third sentence asks a question, but it is meant to give an order. Problems are created by this third kind of question in two ways: 1) the sender's intent is unclear because one kind of sentence is used to do another's work; and 2) the language says something other than what the sender intends. ("Can" literally means "do you have the ability to?" This makes the literal meaning of the third sentence, "Are you capable of telling me the time?")

VARIOUS FORMATS FOR GIVING ORDERS

Formats for giving orders are discussed below in three categories: command; suggestion; and instruction.

The command is a direct imperative containing a complete order in the briefest and most straightforward manner possible. The command is frequently used in policing situations and is especially appropriate in emergencies. Specifically, commands stress what to do.

Example—The Command

"Hold your hands above your head."
"Drop that gun."
"Johnson, ride in nine with Kelly."
"D Wing girls fall in."

The suggestion is a command in which the sender softens his language because, in encoding, the sender has decided that a command may be offensive to the receiver. The suggestion takes a different tone than the command but it carries the same authority. It relies on the receiver's cooperation whereas the command relies on implied force. The suggestion stresses what *might* be done.

Example—The Suggestion

"If you'll hold your hands above your head, it will make it easier to search you."

"Why don't you put down that gun, Joe, and then nobody will get hurt."

"If you'll ride to headquarters with Officer Kelly, I'll follow in this car and meet you there."

"If we group up now and walk to the auditorium, we'll be in time for the movie."

Instructions are a series or sequence of commands or procedures which result in an order. Instructions can be given one-to-one, through an intermediary, or in staff meetings. As the number of persons included in the process increases, the focus of instruction giving broadens. Police departments rely heavily on the staff meeting format, discussed below as "briefing sessions." (Note that instructions stress *how* to do it.)

Example—Instruction, "The Briefing Session"

As police officers come on duty in rotating shifts, they are informed of the department's actions during their absence by briefing sessions. These sessions are called by different departments such names as "reading the watch," "fall in," "muster," and "line up."

The officers in the field write up what are usually called "press sheets," accounts of their activities. These press sheets are collected in some central location, such as a squad room, and are available for individual officer's inspection.

Some departments use an indexed briefing folder for press sheets. This folder is organized under subheadings such as Intelligence, Wanted Persons, Investigations, Subpoenas, and M.O.'s. In this way, officers inspecting the folder are directed to pertinent information which falls within their own sphere of responsibility. Some departments use video tape. A department may tape its briefings every twenty-four hours, and then have the sergeant on duty notify the men of any further developments not covered.

A less elaborate, but accurate, system of briefing preparation is through the use of teletype or telex machines. In large urban areas, with a number of precinct houses spread far apart, the teletype machine provides accurate and simultaneous briefings which, again, can be supplemented by the sergeant on duty. The only problem here is making it convenient for all the officers coming on duty to read the briefing within a relatively short period of time.

In most departments, however, it is the traditional reading of the watch which structures the briefing session. Rotating the reading of the watch gives each officer, in turn, the experience of leading the briefing session. This system brings officers together and gives each a sense of significance within the organizational structure.

WHO IS RESPONSIBLE FOR THE MESSAGE?

Giving orders is encoded communication based entirely on the sender's concept of the action to be taken. This is different from communication in which encoding is linked to responding, as in the interview. Only where encoding includes both the sender's concept and the receiver's last transmission is the responsibility for the message shared. The sender, as leader, enforces his concept by encoding and transmitting an order. This makes the sender entirely responsible for the message.

WHAT IS THE STYLE OF CONTROL?

Sole responsibility is the essence of authority. Therefore, the sender's responsibility for the message sets an authoritarian tone for the order. This can, however, be softened if the suggestion format is chosen rather than the command format.

WHAT KIND OF TIME IS NEEDED?

Orders are often more effective if they are brief. Carefully encoded suggestions and commmands which are quickly transmitted and absorbed are likely to produce the desired impact. Similarly, instructions should be condensed so they may be more readily received and retained.

HOW ARE GOALS FORMULATED?

Orders transmit the sender's goals. There is no participation between sender and receiver in formulating goals.

HOW APPARENT IS FEEDBACK?

The brief, authoritarian imperative does not encourage feedback. Because of the pressure typical of order-giving situations, senders may not devote much attention to presentation. In these circumstances, receivers may not feel that their feedback is desired. If, however, senders are to be sure that their order giving is effective, they must seek feedback when pressures are lifted.

WHAT IS THE ROLE OF FEEDBACK?

To become consistently clear and accurate in giving orders, the sender must be aware of feedback. With each transmission of orders, the sender may adjust the presentation of further orders in an effort to move the receiver closer to the desired responses. In making these adjustments, the sender may choose to work on areas listed in the checklists below.

I—Accuracy Checklist

A. Who is involved? What people?
B. What is involved? What objects and events?
C. How many are involved?
D. When? At what time?
E. Where? At what place?
F. In what way? By what method?
G. ("Why" is usually included with these kinds of questions. However, it may not always be appropriate in giving orders.)

II—Clarity Checklist

A. Right word. (Have I chosen words which mean precisely what I want to say?)
B. Exact word. (Have I chosen the most specific words?)
C. Confusing word. (Have I avoided words which might mislead?)
D. Confusing sequence. (Did I organize my ideas so that they are easy to follow?)
E. Jargon. (Did I avoid slang and words which only a special group might know?)

REVISING ORDERS

On the basis of the feedback the sender receives, he can use the accuracy checklist and the clarity checklist to work on giving more effective orders.

Example—Revising Orders

1. Ineffective: "Jack, I want your guys around City Hall before those big wigs leave today."

   Effective: "Jack, I want six of your men at the three Main Street exits of City Hall between 2:30 and 3:30 this afternoon before the union leaders leave."

2. Ineffective: "That Johnson kid's probably lying. Prints all over the car—no owner record. Let's check Connors."

   Effective: "Johnson's story doesn't hold up. The print report shows somebody else's prints all over the car. Check to see if they match Connors'; he reported a car fitting this description missing. The lot owner Johnson named has no record of selling him a car."

The following chart lists each change made in revising these examples. The "reference" column tells which items on the accuracy and clarity checklists were used in making these changes. Following the chart is an explanation of how these revisions worked.

Example—Revising Orders Using the Checklists

Change	Checklist Reference
Example 1	
"your guys" to "*six* of your *men*"	I.C.; II.B.
"*around* City Hall" to "*three Main Street exits of* City Hall"	I.E.; II.C.
"*before* those big wigs leave *today*" *to* "*between 2:30 and 3:30 this afternoon* before the union leaders leave"	I.D.; II.A.; II.E.
Example 2	
"probably *lying*" to "*story doesn't hold up*"	II.C.
"*prints* all over the car" to "report shows *somebody else's prints*"	I.A.; II.C.
"no *owner record*" to "no *record of selling*"	I.B.; II.A.
"Connors" to "reported a car . . . missing"	I.F.; II.D.

In the first example, "your guys" wasn't specific. "Six of your men" answers the question, "How many?" "Around City Hall" is misleading: does the sender want the men to circle the building? to be in its vicinity? "At the three Main Street exits" answers the question, "Where?" "Before those big wigs leave today" assumes that the receiver knows just when those in question are leaving. The use of "big wigs" is jargon; the receiver may not recognize those so labelled. Union leaders clears the matter. "Between 2:30 and 3:30 this afternoon" answers the question, "When?"

In the second example, "lying" is a confusing word. Does Johnson lie all the time, or only in a particular instance? In what way is he lying? His story not "holding up" specifies the problem. The use of "prints" in "prints all over the car" is misleading. Whose prints? The revision explains. "Owner record" was the wrong word: it did not accurately answer the question, "What is involved?" The reference to "Connors" is first presented in a sequence which makes it impossible to know how he fits into the problem described. The revision explains Connors' role, answering the question, "In what way?"

RESPONDING TO MISINTERPRETATION

Even where orders are clear and accurate, there is always the possibility of misinterpretation and, consequently, a break-down in communication. The following are procedures for responding to misinterpretation.

First, do not become angry. It is useless to blame the receiver for misinterpretation. It takes two to create communication difficulties.

Second, do not repeat the order word for word. Repetition can be interpreted as an insult. If the message is misinterpreted, reword the ordering by keeping in mind the considerations listed in the accuracy and clarity checklists.

Third, try to view your order as if you were the receiver. You have two resources in doing this: 1) your experience of the receiver, and 2) his restatement of the misinterpreted message. If you can see it his way, you can revise the message so that your meaning comes through.

Fourth, in sending the message, make it clear that you expect to be understood the first time. If your expectations are pessimistic, you are likely to fluster the receiver so that his concentration on your message will be diverted.

SUMMARY

This chapter contrasted giving orders with interviewing. It discussed giving orders in terms of the type of transmission used, responsibility for the message, style of control, time needs, goal formulation, and feedback. It presented accuracy and clarity checklists for revising orders. Finally, it suggested ways of both avoiding and responding to misinterpretation.

Discussion Questions

1. This chapter begins with a chart listing the differences between interviewing and giving orders. How does each item relate to the five steps in the communication model (Chapter 1)?
2. What is the role of giving orders in advertising? How does this compare with the use of giving orders in law enforcement work?
3. From basic arithmetic through the most complicated mathematical computation, all quantitative procedures include methods for checking accuracy. How do these compare with the procedures presented in this chapter for checking clarity and accuracy when giving orders?

Exercises

1. In a magazine or newspaper look for advertisements which use each of the formats for giving orders: command, suggestion, instruction.
2. Keep a diary for one day. Accurately record the words you use in your imperatives.
3. Review your diary:
   a. What format does each order take?
   b. Rewrite each in a different format. In its new form, would it do the job as well?
   c. How could each be improved by using the accuracy checklist?
   d. How could each be improved by using the clarity checklist?

CHAPTER 6

INTERPERSONAL RELATIONSHIPS

Feelings, attitudes, and past experiences play a major role in our relationship with others.

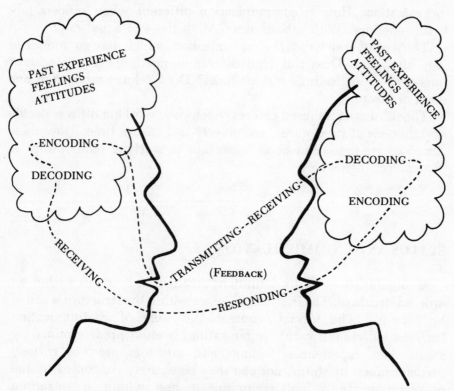

**THE ROLE OF
PAST EXPERIENCE, FEELINGS AND ATTITUDES IN
THE COMMUNICATION MODEL**

A theoretical discussion of what motivates people while encoding and decoding belongs in a psychology text. The skills presented in this text emphasize communication with others, rather than looking in at oneself. For this reason, this chapter is arranged as a discussion of three kinds of circumstances in which law enforcement officers are likely to be aware of the interaction of communication and past experiences, feelings and attitudes.

The first area discussed is status and its role within the organization. How is communication different when officers talk with superiors? With subordinates? With those of equal rank?

The second area is casual communication, which may go unnoticed day after day. Does this kind of communication carry important messages about feelings and attitudes? Does it have more than one level of meaning?

The third area is shared choices. Each day, working officers decide together about procedures, use objects and leisure time. How these decisions are made can be as important to working relationships as the choices themselves.

STATUS AND COMMUNICATION

An organization, by its definition, arranges individuals within an ordered structure. The individual's place within the structure is called his "status." The format, content and tone of communication between individuals within organizations is often predetermined by status. Past experiences, feelings and attitudes are not entirely predetermined by status, nor can they be entirely controlled by the organization. Individuals communicate best within organizations when they are aware enough of the communication process to express freely their feelings and attitudes while still remaining consistent with their status role.

The structural model for some justice administration organizations is the social service agency. The predominately informal structure for communication within such organizations will often allow feelings and attitudes to be expressed. In para-military justice administration organizations, such as police departments, communication may be much more formal, especially between officers of different ranks. Nonetheless, underlying feelings and attitudes will, in part, determine the result of the communication.

RELATING TO SUPERIORS AND SUBORDINATES

The way in which an individual relates to his superiors and subordinates within an organization is influenced by past experience, feelings and attitudes toward authority figures. Authority figures are those people whose status allows them to tell the individual what to do. In childhood, typical authority figures are parents and teachers.

Attitudes toward authority figures are formed as children develop. Children learn how to be authority figures from those who have control over them. These attitudes formed in childhood will, to a great extent, determine basic attitudes toward superiors, and also later toward subordinates.

The basic superior/subordinate relationship in a police department is the relationship between "rookies" and their training officers. "Rookies" are new recruits to a police department. Training officers, as teachers and higher ranking officers, are authority figures.

The feelings and attitudes rookies reveal in their communication with training officers are attitudes toward authority figures. Where comfortable and productive patterns have been learned in relating to parents and teachers, rookies will relate well to training officers—communication is likely to be smooth. Where early experiences with authority figures were frightening or frustrating, rookies are likely to have problems adjusting to their new relationship with training officers.

Training officers learned how to be authority figures by watching their parents and teachers as they were growing up. Where parents and teachers provided good models, (consistent, supporting, protecting) training officers are likely to show the same traits. Where models were poor (arbitrary, competitive, uncaring), problems are likely to arise in the training officers' performance as communicators.

Individuals in subordinate status positions are unlikely to change communication between superiors and subordinates within a police organization. Para-military structure requires subordinates to react to communication from superiors, not to analyze it. Understanding this restricted communication may not lead to any change, but it develops an awareness which is useful in other, less restricted, circumstances.

RELATING TO THOSE OF EQUAL RANK

Within a police department, where organizational status is determined by official rank, relationships with superiors and subordinates will exhibit communication which is different from communication with those of equal rank. The most important aspect of communication between those of equal rank is that true feelings and attitudes can be expressed openly and real needs can be made evident. This kind of communication between officers of equal rank creates trust and a relaxed working environment.

Police officers working in pairs have a great investment in communicating effectively. That is, each partner must depend on the other's support in carrying out assignments. Often, an officer's life will depend on his partner.

The personal relationship between the officers is also an important aspect of their communication. Partners do not necessarily have to like each other to work well together. They may remain cool toward each other as individuals, while still functioning effectively within the police unit. However, it is to each individual's advantage if the relationship between partners can be friendly. Partners inevitably spend a good deal of time together when relatively little is happening. They frequently eat together. Friendliness between them can create a counterbalance to the stress of police work and can strengthen their effectiveness as a team.

Friendly communication is a form of recreation. It relaxes and amuses. When friendly communication characterizes relationships, law enforcement officers will take longer to become fatigued. Their friendly communication will provide on-going recreation. When stress situations do occur, they will be better able to handle them than officers for whom cold and distant personal relationships have failed to relieve the tensions of duty.

When officers are functioning in groups of equal rank, they are said to be functioning as "peer groups." Peer groups may be based on common economic status, common achievement levels or common social status. Within police departments, peer groups are usually formed on the basis of common age category and common rank range.

Peer group communications are usually characterized by warmth and ease. Peers are usually more comfortable and open when talking to each other than when they are talking to superiors or subordinates. It is important to the peer group, however, that its members maintain the boundaries of the group. That is, peers must not try to out-class one another or take charge, unless, of course, they want to leave the group.

Boundaries become most apparent when cliques develop within peer groups. A "clique" is an exclusive group of peers. Based on some arbitrary selection process, cliques actively exclude certain people. Communications between members of a clique are uniquely warm, but often secretive as well. It is important to clique members to share something which is unavailable to those outside the clique. For this reason, clique communications are likely to make heavy use of "in" expressions, private jokes, and conspiratorial winks.

Cliques are very likely to arise within the peer groupings of a police department. Their presence creates problems. Because cliques are based on exclusiveness, the communications of clique members are likely to create feelings of rejection in non-members. Where officers must work together under conditions of stress, cliques may create hostilities.

CASUAL COMMUNICATION: OVERT AND COVERT MESSAGES

Casual communication includes those transmissions for which we spend very little time consciously encoding. It is easy to assume that we are not thinking (encoding) as we exchange greetings or tease and joke with co-workers. Techniques of communication analysis which permit decoding secondary meanings from these seemingly simple transmissions reveal their importance for working relationships within law enforcement organizations.

A basic technique for analyzing these transmissions is distinguishing between overt and covert meaning. Overt meaning is indicated by actual content; covert meaning is determined by such things as nonverbals (including tone of voice) and secondary information.

Example—Covert and Overt Meaning

Transmission: "Thank you for not smoking."

Overt message: "I am pleased that you have chosen not to smoke."

Covert meaning: "You're doing it my way. I hate cigarette smoke. I win."

Transmission: "Now that you're here, Tony, we can begin the meeting."

Overt message: "We can start because you're here."

(Nonverbals accompanying this transmission were drumming fingers, clipped tone, no eye contact, furrowed brow, tight lips, and shuffling papers.)

Covert meaning: "You've held us up."

Transmission: "Why don't you drive today, MacAffrey?"

Overt message: "Would you drive today?" (Secondary information: in this particular department, the lower ranking officer always drives; the senior officer always rides.)

Covert meaning: "I don't respect you."

A second technique for analyzing these transmissions is looking for double messages. These are transmissions in which the distinction between overt and covert is blurred so that the receiver may have some difficulty in understanding which message he should follow.

Example—Double Message Analysis

Transmission: "OK, go ahead and dispense with that procedure if you really think it's all right."

There are two ways to decode this message. One is, "Yes, do dispense with the procedure." Another is, "No, don't dispense with the procedure."

Greetings

As working officers greet one another, they also communicate feelings and attitudes. Of course, the most easily detected greeting attitude is respect. This is usually indicated by including "sir," as in "Good morning, sir." This address is used, in most instances, when greeting superiors.

When those of equal rank greet one another, there is more room for varied expression. Greetings which express liking are often more the function of non-verbals than content. Most people can tell the difference between a friendly and a cold greeting even if identical words are used for each.

Greetings between officers become communication problems when humor enters the greeting. Greetings which are well meant but which take the format of teasing or joking cannot be relied on to communicate intent. For example, Tom on entering the department is greeted by "Hey there, Tom, you goof off!" Tom may not like being called a goof off. However, he may conceal his resentment because law enforcement etiquette usually places a high value on being able to take good natured kidding.

Joking and Teasing

Officers often work under hazardous conditions where dangers are usually hidden until they emerge full force. Under these conditions, officers must function as part of a closely coordinated unit. Teasing and joking, especially in American society, have the traditional value of indicating good fellowship within groups. This value places greatest emphasis on the appearance of good fellowship.

Psychologists tell us that teasing and joking can reduce anxieties. In a law enforcement context, teasing and joking often alleviate tension that builds up during stress periods. However, psychologists also tell us that the surface humor of teasing and joking can conceal resentment. That is, joking and teasing not only ease tension, but they may also express dislikes and resentments which cannot be aired because of the great emphasis on the appearance of good fellowship.

Example—Joking and Teasing

Bill and John are in the locker room, changing from street clothes to their uniforms.

Bill: "How's that old clunker of yours doing, John boy."

John: "Needs a valve job."

Bill: "It'll take more than that to keep that mess running."

John: "Well, Bill, I guess it's relatively the same age you are."

Bill: "I don't need no valve job, man. I'm in better shape than any of you punk kids any day."

On the surface, tone of voice and manner would suggest to an observer that this is a good-natured exchange between men who know each other well and must work together under difficult conditions. However, there may be more to their communication than this.

Though Bill's initial comment may have been well intended, it could have been perceived by John as a criticism. John may feel some resentment at hearing his car referred to as an "old clunker," especially at a time when he is considering a further investment in the car's maintenance. Though he is younger than Bill, he may not take the term "boy" to express an older man's affectionate gruffness with a younger man. John may resent being called "boy." Such covert resentments may be the reason for John's terse reply.

Bill, however, sees nothing to deter him from keeping up the joke. He again assaults John's car, this time as a "mess." John's feelings have clearly been hooked: his teasing reply is a criticism of Bill, based on age. Bill's feelings are stung by this assault. He defends himself against the suggestion of getting old by putting down the general category of officers in John's age group.

This exchange may still, of course, be viewed as the harmless joking typical of police locker rooms. However, when communication problems develop among officers, it is wise to consider the possible covert meanings of the joking and teasing that has been involved.

Teasing can be used by officers to test one another's feelings and attitudes. This testing often takes the form of overstating hostility, innocence, stupidity, or wisdom in order to see what the other officer will do. The purpose of the teasing is to probe for responses without seeming to care. This kind of teasing can be difficult to respond to because it sends a double message. On the one hand, it states a position which is usually a challenge; on the other hand, it sends a message which says, "I'm only kidding."

Punctuality

Being on time or not being on time is often indicative of feelings and attitudes about assignments, fellow officers, or organizations. There are, of course, times when circumstances make it impossible to be on time and when an officer is always late, it is useless to blame circumstance.

Chronic lateness, like joking and teasing, can be used to express covert hostility. The covert message is, "I want to punish you by making you wait." Another covert message might be, "I'm avoiding this."

SHARED CHOICES

When officers work in teams or in groups, their police task is what they talk about. However, they share other areas of communication which are likely to shape the effectiveness of their working relationship. These areas of shared choices (listed below) communicate, by the way they are handled, what each officer thinks of the other(s).

Shared Choices

Partner Choice

Priorities for Teams

Area Choice

Vehicle Choice

Where to Eat

Leisure Choices

Partner Choice. Choosing a partner expresses a preference, and thereby says (however covertly), "I like you." Choosing a partner also expresses a negative preference by not choosing others as partners. Some individuals may interpret not being chosen as a rejection. They may be unaware of this response themselves, and yet their responses to those by whom they feel rejected may carry the coloration of this resentment.

Priorities for Teams. Where officers structure their own work procedure, the team or the group must arrive at a structure of priorities.

Each member needs to feel that he has had a share in structuring priorities. This participation is important to a cohesive work unit. When individuals feel that their approach has been discounted or dismissed, they are less likely to work effectively toward the goals imposed on them. Their communications are likely to bristle with covert hostility.

Area Choice. When partners are free to choose their work areas, shared choice becomes an important mode of communication. When their preferences match, communication will be smooth. However, officers must also respect each other's differing preferences. Communication will be smooth to the extent that each officer feels that his preference has been recognized and respected.

Vehicle Choice. Partners, or members of a team, may have differing preferences about which vehicle to use (where selection is possible). Again, the relationships between the individuals working together will be in part determined by how such choices are made. The important issue in such choice-making situations is not "who gets his way," but that each individual feels that his preference was respected.

Where to Eat. Perhaps the shared choice which has the deepest effect on the relations and communications between officers is that of choosing where to eat. Eating a meal is one of the few activities during an officer's work day which allows for relaxation and meeting personal needs. Meeting these needs usually must be postponed in the name of duty. For this reason, officers are likely to look forward to a meal and to place importance on where it is eaten.

Children learn early in life to associate mother's love with the food she prepares. That is why so many people like their food cooked the way "mother used to make it." Eating patterns associated with secure, happy moments in childhood are likely to be repeated by the adults.

For this reason, officers' preferences in eating places should be taken seriously. Every effort should be made to see that each officer has ample opportunity to relieve the tensions of law enforcement work and that he participates in choosing the location of that meal.

Leisure Choices. Police officers, as a group, tend to socialize most frequently with other police officers. In making choices for their leisure time, officers naturally look for stress-free encounters. They need recreation in which they are perceived as fun-seeking individuals, not as representatives of organized social power. For this reason, officers are likely to seek each others' company during their leisure hours.

By spending recreational time together, police are communicating to society that they constitute a special social category. Society reacts to this as do the families of police personnel. A policeman's wife, to society, is more often regarded as a *policeman's wife* than just a wife. Also, constant socializing with police families enforces the fact that police and their families must be able to see themselves in terms of a special social category.

To others, the social exclusiveness of police officers may transmit, "We are a special group." Though the group, from the police point of view, may exist because of common work experiences, society may regard it differently. This is because individuals within society are likely to project their feelings about authority onto police officers. They are likely to see police socializing as an expression of superiority. Individuals who fear or resent the police may make an issue of officers relations with one another when they are off duty.

Of course, when officers move out of the police social group into mixed groups, they experience tensions which are not present within the police group. However, they also benefit by expanding their own social perceptions. At the same time, opening up the police social sphere gives others in society a chance to see police personnel as people like themselves.

SUMMARY

This chapter discussed the relationship of past experience, feelings and attitudes to communication. The point of view was that of communication outward, rather than psychological analysis inward. The study of communication is not complete without a discussion of past experience, feelings and attitudes because the covert messages involved may carry as much meaning as the accompanying overt messages.

Discussion Questions

1. Many people say that it is useless to look for "hidden meanings" in what we say and what is said to us. Do you agree with this statement?

2. Are the status relationships discussed in this chapter similar to those in a typical high school? Are there similar or different patterns of communication because of the status relationships?

3. How does this chapter's discussion of covert and overt meaning relate to the discussion of nonverbal communication in Chapter 3?

4. What changes do you see in your own communication patterns as you move between situations in which you are an authority figure and situations in which you are acted upon by authority figures?

Exercises

1. Over a period of a few days, list statements which you interpret as having both overt and covert messages.

2. Have a few members of the class act out a shared-choice situation similar to those described in this chapter. The rest of the class, as observers, should note the following:

   a. Who dominates the decision making process?
      Who is not fully included?

   b. At what points in the discussion does the difference in participation become evident?

   c. What specific changes would result in a decision in which all had participated fully?

3. In magazines, newspapers or on television look for advertisements which attempt to persuade. List both the overt and covert messages in the ad.

CHAPTER 7

LANGUAGE USE

In the last chapter, we discussed the role of past experience, feelings and attitudes in communication. This chapter discusses social and cultural influences on communication.

As people of other nations have entered American society, they have had to adjust their own culture and language heritage to the American experience. At the same time, they have had to adjust to American reaction to their presence in American society. In this process they have developed dialects of American English.

As American society has grown, its attitudes toward certain life styles have forced special groups to see themselves as apart from society. These special groups have had to adjust to social responses ranging from dislike to arrest. Their special argot has emerged from their adjustment process.

DIALECTS

Dialect is a variety of language spoken by a specific group which is identifiable by geographic, social, ethnic, historic, life style or religious characteristics. A dialect varies in pronunciation, vocabulary, and grammar from other varieties of the same language.

Speech communities, formed of people united by dialect, have their own patterns of language. Although these language patterns may be unfamiliar, it is necessary to comprehend and respect these language systems as whole and logical. It can be shown that the "rules" of most dialects are consistently observed; linguists study them as whole systems. Many of the dialects an officer experiences daily are spoken by a larger percent of the population than that which speaks the officer's own dialect. Some American dialects date from the Colonial period of our history.

Example—The Black American Speech Community

The Black American community has its origins in slavery. Black slaves had a great need for privacy in circumstances where communications were heavily scrutinized by white masters. This need gave rise to a slave dialect of English which allowed the slaves to talk with each other without being understood by the master.

Following the prohibition of slavery, Black Americans remained in the South as farmers and servants. The hostility of the dominant white population forced a continuation of the slave dialect by now free blacks. As Black people moved from the rural South to the urban North and West, they found themselves forced into ghettoes by the hostility and discrimination of the white community.

In terms of language theory, Black urban dialect is very much like the Black rural dialect of the slaves and freedmen. It uses relatively few words; it depends on a limited vocabulary. The use of plurals is restricted; the past tense is modified. Changes from formal usage occur in grammar and word order.

Words and phrases change meaning as they pass from the traditional language to the special dialect. One common way that this change occurs is in reversal of honorific (positive) and pejorative (negative) values, switching the good and bad connotations of an expression. For example, when a Black man says of a woman, "She's bad," he means that she has valuable attributes such as beauty, charm, intelligence or style. He switches the honorific value of the word "good" to its usually pejorative opposite, "bad."

Although it is traditional, some Black dialect is a vernacular (slang) of expressions which change frequently. By the time these phrases have worked their way into the wider vernacular, they are out of fashion with Blacks.

In ordinary conversation, the word dialect often connotes a "corrupt" form of language. This is not necessarily true. Studies of the origins of languages show that a predominant language grows out of a collection of original dialects. This standardization grows out of a desire for community, often at the national level.

In the United States, no one dialect of American English has become the recognized national Standard. Regional dialects have become more and more intermingled as American society has become mobile and media-educated. However, American English did go through certain formalization processes. American "primers" of the seventeenth, eighteenth and nineteenth centuries promoted standard-ized language patterns. These little books' primary purpose was to teach children how to spell and read in preparation for Bible study. But the effect on language was to standardize it. Noah Webster's *Dictionary* and the growth of printing and distribution channels in the early nineteenth century encouraged a standardized formal language.

Because of the United States' many nationalities, no one spoken dialect predominates. Even differences in intonation are not especially distinctive between regions of the United States. The American English speaker can readily understand the Harvard accent, the Utah twang, and the western drawl. The dialects of these special speech communities add color, not standards, to our language.

Linguistic geographers divide the United States into three main dialect areas: northern, midland and southern. Dialects are most clearly distinguishable on the Atlantic coast where they reflect the original colonial settlement patterns. The farther west we go, the more the dialect areas blend. The three dialect areas are differentiated by pronunciation, vocabulary, and grammar.

FUNCTIONAL DIALECTS: PIDGIN, CREOLE, AND PATOIS

When two groups of people speaking different languages are forced to talk together, they invent a pidgin language, also called a creolized language or patois. The pidgin is not the native language of either group; it is a mixed language. One language supplies a simplified version of its grammar into which is inserted some of the vocabulariy of the other.

The ancient pidgin underlying Black Nonstandard dialects originated on the west African coast. Some of the these African languages include Twi, Hausa, Ibo, Yoruba. In the United States, later generations of Blacks spoke this pidgin as their creole mother tongue—their native and only language.

This creole influence is still slightly retained in modern Black Nonstandard dialects and is reflected especially in its verb system, even though its vocabulary is mostly English. One example of Black creole English which still exists today is Gullah, the language spoken by Blacks in the Carolina Sea islands and the coastal regions of South Carolina, Georgia and Northeastern Florida.

ARGOTS

In addition to geographic division of dialects in the United States, we can see some social divisions of dialects. Regular patterns of language differences identify social groups. The languages are regular and the differences defining social levels are clear. These social dialects are called "argots."

In many large cities, certain ethnic, economic, age and life style minorities avoid formal language patterns. The argots they speak instead are a specialized dialect in which a unique vocabulary used by a particular group forms a speech community. Argots also function as "secret" codes known only to the initiates of the particular speech community.

CULTURAL CONCEPTS

Behind the language changes which create dialect lie the cultural concepts which grow from a group's past experience. These cultural concepts shape feelings and attitudes. When individuals from different dialect speech groups communicate, difficulty may arise from their unrecognized differences in cultural concepts. These concepts include strongly felt judgments about how private life and the larger society should be conducted. Officers who fail to examine their own cultural concepts and who do not understand the cultural concepts of others, will experience communication difficulties.

Example—LaMordida

This is one cultural concept which creates communication difficulty when law enforcement officers deal with *chicanos* and *latinos*. In some parts of Latin America, a change in government means a change in police staff. For this reason, some Latin American police officers often commit graft during their relatively brief term of office. The poor and uneducated experience this police corruption as *la mordida*, the bite. Their experience in their own country is likely to color their expectations of American police.

When communicators examine their own, and others', cultural concepts, they may find more points in common than expected.

Example—Machismo

This is a cultural concept which can create difficulties in communicating with *chicanos* and *latinos*, if it is not understood. However, when the concept is looked at closely, it turns out to have much in common with the attitudes of many American speech communities.

Throughout Latin American culture runs the vitally important concept of "machismo," the ideal of masculinity. In simple language, machismo means that every man, no matter how humble, has a precious masculine honor to protect. To his wife, the *latino* or *chicano* "macho" is king; to his family he is absolute authority. His machismo keeps him ever-vigilant against any insult to his masculine honor. When women are present, *latino* or *chicano* men are concerned not only with communicating with others but also with maintaining the respect of the women present by preserving masculine honor.

JUDGMENTS BASED ON LANGUAGE USE

Development and change in a language does not occur without corresponding social reactions. Often these reactions occur as judgments about individuals based on their use of dialect or argot.

It is not uncommon for members of a particular speech community to feel that their dialect or argot is superior to any other. In language communities where there is a Standard, snobbery may be based on proper use of the Standard or closeness of a dialect to the Standard. In American English, where there is no Standard, there is still a strong tendency for speech communities to see their own patterns as better than those of other speech communities.

Judgments based on language use are often tied to judgments based on race, national origin or life style. The way an individual uses American English may awaken or reinforce a listener's prejudices. Assumptions about the merit of a particular dialect may affect assumptions about the merit of an individual. Such judgments based on language use interfere with the decoding and encoding processes. If assumptions about the sender are based on his speech patterns alone or on a cluster of secondary data which also includes dress, skin color, and mannerisms, the decoding process will be distorted. The response will reflect this distortion and is likely to be inappropriate.

SUMMARY

Dialects and argots of American English have developed as American society has grown and changed. Each group (national origin, race, religion, life style) contributing to this growth and change has also contributed cultural concepts. Some of these concepts create barriers to communication; others provide a common ground for communicators. Judgments based on language use, influence encoding and decoding in the same way cultural concepts do. In both cases, assumptions must be explored and discussed if communication is to be complete.

Discussion Questions

1. What personal judgments have you based on other people's language use? Analyze the distortion in encoding and decoding that this has created?
2. What is the role of language use differences in social problems? Illustrate your answer with a current problem.
3. Would you consider professional jargon an argot? Why?

Exercises

1. Dialects have contributed many foreign words to the English language. See if your class can list twenty-five words and the foreign languages from which they came.
2. Describe yourself as a member of two or more language use groups. Consider such factors as age, life style, ethnic and racial background.

CHAPTER 8

STRATEGIES FOR
WRITTEN COMMUNICATION

One of the hardest tasks in writing is getting started. Getting started means encoding a written message.

Equally difficult is *not* always writing the same way. This means adopting a different approach, or strategy, for different messages.

This chapter deals with specific writing strategies, called "rhetorical concepts," first developed by ancient Greek and Roman thinkers. These strategies give the writer alternatives from which to choose. They help the writer get started and they help break repetitive patterns.

Chapter Two presented these same kind of strategies for oral communication. The four strategies discussed here are exposition, argumentation, description, and narration. The discussion of each of these four strategies will include brief examples. After each strategy has been fully discussed, we will utilize that strategy in preparing a typical college writing assignment. This will be a paper on "Crisis Intervention Training for Police Personnel."

EXPOSITION

Exposition is a way of ordering experience. It moves from experience to idea. Exposition explains logical relationships.

There are six ways of using the expository strategy in written communication. They are defining, illustrating, comparing and contrasting, classifying, analyzing and time ordering.

DEFINING

Defining is an important strategy for writing because it clarifies particular meanings and reduces the distortion arising from the different definitions each of us has for exactly the same words. Definition depends on an individual's past experience, beliefs and attitudes. Definition specifies ideals or concepts which writer and reader can share.

Defining does not necessarily mean dictionary definitions. Dictionary definitions are only the beginning of meaning. This is because meaning comes from context.

Definition is especially important when a writer is working from general ideas to specifics. The writer needs to define terms so that his reader can follow his intended purpose. If writers fail to provide necessary definitions, messages are likely to be misinterpreted. Without the aid of specific definitions, the audience will be unable to follow the logic and meaning of the message. Concepts left at an abstract level often seem vague or ambiguous to the reader. Definition, as a writing strategy, not only helps clarify the meaning and the point of reference, but also helps writers grasp their material.

Example—Defining

This area is relatively free of plant pests. By "relatively free" I mean that there are only two kinds of plant pests native to the area.

As writers define, they find that they understand better what they are saying.

ILLUSTRATING

Illustrating presents the reader with specific examples of concepts. Illustrations can be anecdotal, metaphorical, and direct.

Anecdotal illustrations tell a story built around the concept being discussed.

Example—My dorm room provides the privacy I must have to succeed in college. Last week, before a midterm, I studied for thirty-six hours there, and no one disturbed me.

Metaphoric illustrations make the reader see the writer's point of view through poetic or symbolic language.

Example—My dorm room provides the privacy I must have to succeed in college. It is my fort, my private library, my mansion, my ivory tower.

Direct illustrations demonstrate the concept. In this textbook, many concepts are immediately followed by a direct illustration (a sentence, clause or phrase demonstrating the particular concept in action).

> *Example*—My dorm room provides the privacy I must have to succeed in college. Here is a picture of my room showing its private entry and the material I have assembled in it to use when I am studying.

Whichever kind of illustration is used, the most important thing is to clearly illustrate the concept. The goal of illustrative writing is to clarify concepts through the use of examples.

COMPARING AND CONTRASTING

Comparing and contrasting is a strategy of exposition which differentiates between concepts. The writer compares and contrasts concepts by, showing similarities and differences.

Example

> Social science students visit a number of helping institutions. Journalism students visit a number of newspaper and magazine offices. Both groups of students visit Night Court. Social science students find it depressing; journalism students find it exciting.

CLASSIFYING

Classifying organizes ideas together under a major idea to help the reader understand sub-ideas. Classifying groups of sub-ideas can be done in many different ways. Each use of classifying as a writing strategy means beginning with an outline. Each sub-section of the outline becomes a topic to be discussed in the writing. (Some writers try to anticipate that they will write at least a paragraph on each sub-section.) The following examples suggest three ways in which a writer might use classifying to organize a report on a police department.

Classifying, as a writing strategy, reveals the way in which you perceive an idea. It helps your reader understand a simple and clear division of a complex subject into its more simple components. Any classification is arbitrary; some classifications may be more common or easier to understand than others. Conventional ways of classifying can become trite. Then they actually take away from meaning. Innovative ways of classifying can lead to a new awareness of relationships.

Example—Functional Groupings

- A. Administration
- B. Public relations
- C. Citizens' review board
- D. Investigation
    1. Homicide
    2. Larceny
    3. Vice
- E. Patrol
    1. Traffic
    2. Juvenile
    3. First Aid
    4. Districts

Example—Physical Attribute Groupings

These organize sub-ideas by distinctive physical attributes.

- A. Officer Age Groups
    1. 21-25
    2. 26-29
    3. 30-34
    4. 35-39
    5. 40-44
    6. 45-49
    7. 50-60
- B. Officer Height Groups
    1. 5'7"-5'10"
    2. 5'10-½"-6'
    3. 6'½"-6'2"
    4. 6'2-½"-6'4"
    5. 6'4-½"+

C.   Officer Weight Groups
1.   150-174 lbs.
2.   175-190 lbs.
3.   191-205 lbs.
4.   206-219 lbs.
5.   220-235 lbs.
6.   236 lbs. +

Example—Spatial Groupings

This kind of classification best fits situations where geographic distinctions need to be made.

A.   Patrol District #1
1.   Holly Grove
2.   East Wood
3.   Inglenook
B.   Patrol District #2
1.   North East
2.   High Gate
3.   Walliston
C.   Patrol District #3
1.   Hovermore
2.   Wenly
3.   South Side

ANALYZING

Analyzing also divides an idea into parts. But there is a difference between analyzing the parts of a structure and classifying the parts of a structure. Classifying clusters items with similar characteristics. Analyzing, though it divides into parts, never loses sight of the whole structure. Each of the parts in the analysis interrelate and support one another. If we look at a subject, first by classifying the parts and then by analyzing the parts, we come up with two different kinds of statements.

DIFFERENCES BETWEEN CLASSIFYING AND ANALYZING, "ECOLOGY"

Example—Classification

Take five plants at random in a garden. Separate them into some arbitrary classification such as leaf structure.

plants with solid green leaves
plants with spotted leaves
plants with striped leaves
plants with red leaves

There is no inherent interrelationship among the items in the classification scheme; no one item is necessarily important to the other things within its class. Any of the items could be removed and we would still end up with classes of things.

On the other hand, consider an ecological cycle and analyze some of the parts that contribute to the whole. For example, consider the inter-relationships of a coastal oceanographic environmental system. The four elements in the particular system we want to discuss are the sea otter, the kelp, the sea urchin, and the abalone.

Each of the four elements is an integral part of a structure. They are involved in a single shelter and food chain. The sea otter makes his home in the floating kelp. The sea otter's favorite food is the abalone. But the sea otter eats the sea urchin and thus controls the sea urchin population. The sea urchin eats the kelp. Removing any one of these items will upset the balance of their inter-relationship. If man hunts the sea otter, and the sea otter population decreases, the sea urchins increase and destroy the kelp beds. Another way that the system can be upset is that the sea otter may deplete the supply of abalone. He will then move on to other areas, thus vacating the kelp beds himself and allowing the sea urchin to destroy the kelp beds. It is the relationship among the parts which, when analyzed, is responsible for establishing structure.

Example—Crime Analysis

Crimes are classified according to time periods during a given shift, in order to organize a report on that shift's crime activity.

I. HOMICIDES.   II. THEFTS.

A. Homicides 1600-1830.   A. Thefts 1600-1830

B. Homicides 1831-2130.   B. Thefts 1831-2130

C. Homicides 2131-2400.   C. Thefts 2131-2400

This classification organizes occurrences and may be useful for statistical purposes, but it tells nothing of the nature of these crimes. Removing the information regarding thefts 1831-2130 will in no way alter the information about thefts at other times (although it will, of course, throw off the over all picture.)

A rape may be analyzed, in outline form, in the following manner:

I.   The rapist as socially maladjusted.
    A.   Latent hostilities
        1.   Toward women
        2.   Toward racial groups
    B.   Related criminal goals
        1.   Theft
        2.   Assault
II. The rapist as sexually maladjusted
    A.   Fear of women
    B.   Fear of parents
    C.   Misunderstanding victim

Not all of these elements are relevant to every rape. However, in discussing the crime of rape, it is necessary to discuss all of these issues and others as well.

TIME ORDERING

Time ordering is simply retelling something in the time order in which it occurred. It is probably one of the easiest strategies to use.

It deals with cause and effect relationships. What happens first is usually the cause. What comes later is usually the effect.

Example—Time Ordering

Random Order: He shot his wife on Christmas Eve. She'd been running around with the next door neighbor for months. He'd known about it, but kept quiet. That day someone teased him about it at work.

Chronological Order: Suspect says that he knew for some months of an illicit relationship between his wife and their next door neighbor. The day of the incident, while at work, suspect was teased by a fellow employee about this relationship. That evening (Christmas Eve) suspect confronted his wife with the issue. He says that an argument ensued during the course of which he shot her.

The second example uses time ordering which clearly shows cause and effect relationships. Because the affair was going on for some time, the suspect/husband was sensitive about it. Because he was sensitive about it, he was upset by a fellow employee's teasing. Because he was upset, he began an argument with his wife. Because he was arguing and upset about a sensitive issue, he shot his wife.

Here are some words which introduce cause:

> since
> because
> if
> when.

Here are some words which introduce effect:

> therefore
> as a result
> thus
> consequently.

These words do not always appear in cause and effect pairs; one of them may be understood. If a cause word is used, there may not always be an effect word, and vice versa.

Example—Cause and Effect Words

Cause Introduction: Because the street was unlighted, it had a high incidence of muggings.

Effect Introduction: The street was unlighted and therefore had a high incidence of muggings.

USING THE EXPOSITORY STRATEGY

Here are alternative possibilities for beginning to write a paper on "Crisis Intervention Training for Police Personnel."

Defining—Crisis intervention is a new concept in the helping professions. Crisis intervention training focuses on intense and dangerous conflict. It teaches methods of defusing such situations.

Illustrating—Crisis intervention teams have proved their worth on this campus. Last semester, when a sophomore student threatened to commit suicide, it was one such team which talked her into seeking therapy. The crisis intervention team was a buoy without which she would have drowned.

Comparing and contrasting—Crisis intervention teams work with patients in the midst of their environments; hospitals remove patients from their environments. Crisis intervention teams, like probation departments, try to keep the individual working within his real world setting.

Classifying
I.   Frequent types of crises.
    A.   Parent-child conflicts.
    B.   Spouse conflicts.
    C.   Multi-family conflicts.
    D.   Drug and alchohol overdoses.
    E.   Suicide attempts.

Analyzing—Crisis intervention is part of a total community mental health plan. It cooperates closely with such agencies as 1) mental health facilities; 2) juvenile and adult probation departments; 3) other police departments; 4) corrections facilities; and 5) welfare agencies.

Time ordering—This paper will discuss the content of each week of instruction, showing its relation to the over all goal of the police department within the community.

ARGUMENTATION

The difference between argumentation and exposition as modes of communication is important. Exposition presents the subject matter in a straightforward manner with very little value judgment—a *neutral* presentation. Argumentation tries to persuade the reader of a course of action. The argumentative mode is therefore a much more active style of writing. Some of the settings that are appropriate for using an argumentative or persuasive strategy are a news release making an appeal for public support, a political announcement seeking voters' support, and a committee's report seeking approval for its recommendations.

Aristotle, the ancient Greek philosopher, suggested three important parts to persuasion. First, *ethos:* how you get the audience to trust you. Second, *logos:* how to make your arguments appear logical. Third, *pathos:* how well you can play on the audience's emotions. Although Aristotle's comments described formal speechmaking, they are helpful in understanding what makes a presentation persuasive.

Ethos

Persuasion is used to change the behavior of the audience by getting them to follow some particular course of action. Developing credibility with the audience is the job of the first few paragraphs. Here are common examples of ways in which a writer can establish trust with his reader:

> Use language that his audience can understand;
> Start with a simple explanation of his concept and work gradually toward the complexity of it;
> Respect his audience by not making prejudicial remarks;
> Demonstrate knowledge of the subject matter; and
> Indicate sensitivity to the audience's needs.

Logos

The logical development of an argument can follow many patterns. The particular pattern you choose is not as important as your logic. Any of the techniques of exposition can be helpful in setting up a well-organized and logically drawn argument. Logic should emerge from an accurate interrelating of ideas. When organization is logical, the reader can justify the arrangement of ideas and concepts.

PATHOS

Making an appeal to an audience's emotions can be and is often intended to be manipulative.

Example—Coloring the Argument

Positive coloring: Officer Spencer is a seasoned veteran of twenty years' outstanding service in this city's police force. His will be a lonely retirement because of the recent passing of his beloved wife, Mary. This Academy teaching position would be a well-deserved reward for his fine contribution, and would make his retirement years richer.

Negative coloring: Officer Spencer is an older man who will retire after twenty years of mostly satisfactory service in this city's police force. His wife died this year. The Academy teaching job would occupy the extra time created by retirement but it's doubtful if his experience qualifies him for the job.

USING THE ARGUMENTATIVE STRATEGY

Here are three parts of an argument supporting the introduction of crisis intervention training for police personnel:

Ethos: After the recent series of drug overdoses on campus, and the tragic results of two of them, it is not surprising that many students are urging local police to institute crisis intervention training.

Logos: Police are constantly being asked to deal with problems which have traditionally been within the realm of the psychiatrist. Psychiatrists are not available at a moment's notice nor at all times and places. Therefore, police personnel must be trained in the skills first developed by psychiatrists.

Pathos: A defenseless child is being mercilessly beaten by a drunken and enraged parent. An elderly lady has locked herself in a rented room and refuses to come out even though she has not eaten for days. A feud between two families is on the verge of becoming a gun match. Who is to help these people?

DESCRIPTION

Description, as a writing strategy, creates a sharing experience between writer and reader which is both informative and pictorial. In creating this experience, the writer must be aware of his perspective. The writer can be like a camera, an outside eye looking in. Or the writer can perceive the things around him from within the experience. It is best to help the reader clearly understand your perspective.

The advantages of writing about an experience from the perspective of a neutral observer is that the writer can avoid claims of emotional bias. The disadvantage of this objective view is that the writer can become cold and calculating, without sensitivity to people, things and events. The advantage of the subjective approach is its color, emotion, humanness and immediacy. A disadvantage of a subjective description is that the writer may be so overcome with his own personal feelings that he sidesteps, overlooks, or misconstrues significant data.

USING THE DESCRIPTIVE STRATEGY

A paper on crisis intervention training for police personnel might be organized around a visit to a training session. Here are descriptions of such a visit, written from subjective and objective points of view.

> *Objective:* This particular training session worked on sensitivity to others' feelings. Members of the training group talked about their own feelings in relation to the activities of the group.
>
> *Subjective:* This particular training session worked on feelings. How much people experience emotionally! Even when they are only talking about experiences within a training group! Members of the group revealed resentment,

disappointment, exhilaration, strong attachment and disgust resulting from experiences that seemed quite ordinary to me.

NARRATION

Narration presents an understood third person who is responsible for telling the story. The characters and events are only the content; it is up to the narrator to tie things together into logical organization.

A common technique for narrating is to use chronological order. Chronological order re-establishes the event in its particular time sequence. Chronological order makes the reader aware of cause and effect relationships. Because writing in chronological order does not upset what we consider a normal time sequence, suspense is built up as the chronology proceeds.

The writer must be careful about implications of cause and effect relationship. The suspense that naturally builds up using this strategy can lead the audience to misunderstand or misconstrue cause and effect.

Although the writer establishes himself as a third person observer, it is impossible for his own point of view not to show. The reader must understand that this telling of the story is from the writer's point of view.

Using the Narrative Strategy

One section of a paper on crisis intervention training for police personnel might be a narrative of the activities of a typical crisis unit. *Narration:* The crisis intervention team entered the room quietly, one at a time. It is important not to cause alarm. Each team member maintained a position allowing a clear view of all other team members. The team must be able to exchange signals as necessary.

SUMMARY

Writing is a medium for transmitting the message. Writing strategies help the writer in encoding the message. This chapter discussed Exposition, Argumentation, Description, and Narration.

The writer's choice of strategies is based on his assessment of the overall direction of his written message.

Discussion Questions

1. Think of a paper you are now writing, or have recently written. Which strategy did you use? How would your paper have been different if you had chosen one of the other strategies?

2. Many of the distinctions between categories in this chapter are quite subtle. Review the material for a specific definition of the differences between description and narration, classification and analysis, and Anecdotal and Metaphoric Illustrations.

3. Look at the different sections of a newspaper. How does each correspond to the different writing strategies discussed in this chapter?

Exercises

1. This chapter took an imaginary paper on crisis intervention training for police personnel and wrote sections of it corresponding to each of the writing strategies presented. Pick a theme of your own and write a similar set of variations.

2. Review your analysis of writing strategies which correspond to sections of a newspaper. Pick an example of each strategy and rewrite it using another strategy. For what section of the newspaper is it now best suited?

3. Watch television newscasts for strategies of presentation. Be especially aware of argumentation. Do the newscasters stress ethos, logos or pathos?

CHAPTER 9

WRITING THE POLICE REPORT

In the last chapter, we discussed the many possibilities for developing writing based on four strategies: exposition; argumentation; description; and narration. Completion of report forms for justice administration agencies, especially police departments, requires the use of the last of these strategies—narration.

Each justice administration agency has its own version of the short answer report. This report is a form which provides blanks or boxes for specific data. However, all such forms have space for the report writer's narration. As examples, two such forms follow; one is used by a suburban police department, the other by a federal government agency.

Each department has its own standards for the narrative section of the police report. You will learn about these standards from police academy instructors, from superior officers, and from others with whom you work. Their standards will give you an idea of working requirements for writing within your particular organization. This chapter focuses on the best possible writing that can be used in police report writing.

Building the best possible writing habits creates a mental resource for thinking more clearly and expressing thoughts more effectively. Reports written by law enforcement officers are part of the public record. They are carefully analyzed by attorneys, judges, journalists, insurance specialists, private investigators, and any other interested citizens. Therefore, the writers of these reports need to be their own most stringent critics.

ACCURATE PRESENTATION OF DATA

The first job of the police report writer is to accurately present data. This section identifies six areas of data collection.

Names and labels
Time references

Identifying officers
Abbreviations
Continuity
Quotations—direct and indirect

NAMES AND LABELS

Perhaps the most important single detail in the police report is the name of each person involved in the action. Of nearly equal importance are the names or designations of vehicles, weapons, items of evidence, and other specifics that play a significant role in the consequences of the police action reported.

The departmental police report form will include spaces to fill in these names and designations. However, they must appear again in the narrative of the actual event. It is wise to bear in mind that the narrative may be excerpted, in whole or in part, from the completed report form. For this reason, and to insure the accuracy and clarity of a public document, the handling of names and designations should be clear and consistent.

The full name of each person involved should appear in the narrative at the point where he or she first enters the action. Individual departments will specify other information (such as address, or a race and sex abbreviation) which should accompany this first reference.

Further references should avoid the use of the pronouns "he" and "she." These can sometimes lead to wrong interpretations of your account. Use either a shortened form of the complete name, or use labels which will be consistent throughout the report.

Ineffective:	Reporting Officer talked with a man who said he had seen the accident. He said the car was making a right-hand turn.
Effective:	Reporting Officer talked with Mr. Alan Jones, 125 Center St., who said that he had seen the accident. Jones said that the blue car was making a right-hand turn.

or

Effective: Reporting Officer talked with Mr. Alan
(Using Labels) Jones (Witness #1), 125 Center St., who said
                that he had seen the accident. Witness #1
                said that Vehicle #2 was making a
                right-hand turn.

Note that in the ineffective report, Jones was merely noted as "a man," and the blue car as "a car." The specific name, and descriptive data, clarify these references within the report. However, it is usually best to use the system presented in the second effective example, labelling each person and item (Witness #1, Victim #1, Suspect #1, Vehicle #1, Rifle #1, etc.).

TIME REFERENCES

Of major importance in the writing of the report narrative is time reference. Many departments prefer the military system of noting time (0800 hours) to the conventional system (8:00 am). Our concern here is with the words used to modify time references.

The most common practice in police report writing is to use modifiers like "approximately" along with a specific time reference. For example, "Reporting officers responded to the Deluxe Market at approximately 1300 hours." This usage can create problems if the report becomes the focus of a dispute over the facts. How many minutes' range are indicated by the modifier "approximately?" Ten minutes either side of the hour? fifteen? twenty? While this may be an easy reference to clarify when the reference is to the activities of the reporting officers themselves, it becomes more difficult when references are made to the actions of others. For example, "Suspect entered the house at approximately 1300 hours."

The use of a time-range reference eliminates, or at least minimizes, this problem. Time-range references utilize expressions such as "roughly between the hours of" or "sometime between...and...." In this way, the report writer makes it clear that he is estimating time, and that his estimate has specific limits.

Ineffective: Suspects #1 and #2 approached Victim #1 in
                the alley behind the store at approximately
                0900 hours.

Effective: Suspects #1 and #2 approached Victim #1 in
                the alley behind the store sometime between
                0850 and 0910 hours.

Where exact times are known, report writers should include the
source of this accurate knowledge in the report. For example,
"Witness #2 said that she looked at her watch just before waiting on
Suspect #1. She said that it was 6:25 pm."

IDENTIFYING OFFICERS

The examples used in this section refer to the actions of someone
called "reporting officer," instead of "I" or "Sgt. Smith." Each
department has its own particular preference, but as a general rule,
police reports avoid the use of "I" at all times. Instead they refer to the
third person actions of the report writer. Usually, the names of the
officers involved, and of the officer reporting, appear in a special
place on the police report form, rather than in the narrative itself.
Often, this special entry area for the officers' names (and other
identifying data, such as badge number) will also designate the listed
officers by number (Officer #1, Officer #2). Where this is not the case,
it is best to use officers' last names each time they appear in the
narrative.

Ineffective: One officer held the suspect, while another
                searched her for weapons.

Effective: Officer Smith held the suspect, while Officer
                Gomez searched her for weapons.

ABBREVIATIONS

Frequently, the designation "reporting officer" is abbreviated as
"R/O." Each department has its own vocabulary of conventional
abbreviations. These abbreviations are correct in police report
writing, even though they would be incorrect if included in papers
submitted for college courses. Once the writer becomes familiar with
these abbreviations, they save time in report writing; for example,

"R/O met the ambulance at CGH, where it delivered a WMA who was DOA" when you mean "Reporting Officer met the ambulance at County General Hospital, where it delivered a white, male adult who was dead on arrival."

Along with abbreviated words and phrases, it is conventional and expedient in police report writing to shorten sentences by leaving out certain words and phrases that would be expected in well written prose. For the most part, this style of writing will be explained in the police academy, and then again by departmental superiors. As in other instances of report writing style, each department has its own particular preferences. In general, police reports are more likely to read like this:

> R/O responded to a 311, 1122 Jackson Terr., where WMA (later ID as Paul C. Constand, 354 Ovvon Lane, Victim #1) was found uc. He appeared to be victim of a PC1804, with mul. abbr. about the head and arms.

than this

> This reporting officer was asked to come to 1122 Jackson Terrace because it was believed that someone had been seriously injured there. This officer found a white male adult, who was later identified as Mr. Paul C. Constand of 354 Ovvon Lane. He will be hereafter referred to as "Victim Number One." Mr. Constand was unconscious. He appeared to be the victim of a brutal assault, as he had multiple abrasions about the head and arms.

It is the goal of this Chapter that the report writer get the greatest advantage out of this first form of writing by using the communication skills that make the second example easy to understand.

CONTINUITY

Perhaps the surest way to write an ineffective police report is to fail to establish continuity. "Continuity," in the case of police report writing, means creating a sequence of events and details which seems reasonable and clear to the reader. There should be no language in a police report which leads the reader to silently ask questions like "What?" or "Who?"

The easiest way to create continuity is to use chronological order. This means setting things down in the time sequence in which they actually occurred. This will automatically insert data at the point where it first enters the action.

Ineffective: Officer Chow questioned Witness #1 about the missing person's whereabouts. Witness #1 had first made the missing person report. The missing person was Witness #1's neighbor, Mrs. Ethel Cohen, 118 31st St.

Effective: Mrs. Ida Goldman, 112-31st St. (Witness #1), reported her neighbor, Mrs. Ethel Cohen, 118-31st St., as a possible missing person. Officer Chow responded to the home of Witness #1, and questioned her regarding this report.

Of course, there are situations which do not lend themselves to chronological order. When writing a report where it is not possible to put events in chronological order, be on the lookout for a lapse in continuity. Ask yourself as you write: Does this follow logically? Is it clear that these events relate to each other and that this factual data is relevant?

Quotations—Direct and Indirect

Quotations take on special significance in a discussion of police report writing. In conventional writing, authors present quotations for dramatic effect. For example,

Many citizens are asking themselves, "How responsible to public opinion should we expect our elected officials to be?"

When direct quotations enter the public record they are understood to be actual transcriptions of statements made by persons whose names appear in the police report. Therefore, if an officer uses a direct quotation, he must be ready to swear in a court of law that those are exactly the words he heard spoken.

Example—Officer O'Neill responded to 411 Spruce. He was met there by Mrs. Ella Watson who told him, "My no good son beat up my boyfriend."

In this example, Officer O'Neill must be willing to testify that these are Mrs. Watson's exact words. It may be entirely possible for him to do so. But where complications arise, it is best to use alternative forms to introduce quoted material.

Mrs. Watson's words may come to Officer O'Neill second hand, or he may only partially recall them. In either case, he can use forms of quotation that will make the circumstances clear.

If Mrs. Watson's words come second hand, but O'Neill knows and completely recalls the source, the quotation may still be used in its direct form.

Example—Officer O'Neill responded to 411 Spruce. He was met there by Mrs. Mae Jones, 409 Spruce, who said, "My neighbor lady, Mrs. Watson, she called across the way to me saying how her son was beating up on her boyfriend."

If, however, Mrs Watson's words are only remembered in part, it will be best to use the indirect quotation. This is most easily done by describing her statement, rather than quoting it directly.

Example—Officer O'Neill responded to 411 Spruce. He was met there by Mrs. Mae Jones, 409 Spruce, who said that she had been called by her neighbor, Mrs. Ella Watson, 411 Spruce, due to an incident in which her son and a friend were involved in a fight.

Note, however, that this summary of the statement leaves out many possibly important details which the earlier versions included. It is therefore best for the report writer to use key words that he remembers, and to surround these with single quotes. These single quotes indicate that this approximates what was actually said. These single quotes stand for the phrase "words to the effect of."

Example—Officer O'Neill responded to 411 Spruce. He was met there by Mrs. Mae Jones, 409 Spruce, who said that she

had been called by her neighbor, Mrs. Ella Watson, 411
Spruce, who complained that her son was 'beating up on'
her 'boyfriend.'

This example gives more information than the summary which
preceded it. It tells us who Mrs. Watson thought was attacking
whom, and it tells us something about Mrs. Watson's perceived
relationship to the (assumed) victim.

There are instances, however, the phrase "words to the effect of" is
useful. This is especially the case where a police report must include
information to justify a particular police action (for example, forced
entry, as below).

Example—Officers responded to the hotel and heard loud
voices from Room 101 saying words to the effect of 'Help,
he's killing me' and 'I'm going to kill you.' Officers forced
entry into the room.

POLICE REPORT WRITING PROBLEMS

Accurate presentaton of data is not the only requirement of a
well-written police report. The language of the report must be
carefully edited to avoid some common problems of writing style.
These problems include using obscure vocabulary, misplacing
pronouns, proceeding from assumptions, and inadvertently suggest-
ing improper procedure. This section presents ways to avoid these
problems.

AVOIDING OBSCURE VOCABULARY

Working law enforcement officers may become aware of
vocabulary which is unfamiliar to the general public. Their
knowledge of departmental terminology automatically set them off as
possessors of special language. In addition, law enforcement officers
become aware of the vocabularies of the various groups with whom
they deal during the administration of their duties. It is therefore
common for police officers to be aware of many words that have little
or no specific meaning for the layman.

It can be a mistake to include these special words in police reports without, at least, pairing them with common vocabulary words. For example, "Suspect #1 had in his possession a zip gun, a homemade weapon of potentially lethal capability." It is best, however, where possible, to substitute common language for special terminology.

Ineffective: Suspect #3 was wearing black stacks, red bells, green skins and a brown apple hat.

Effective: Suspect #3 was wearing black, high-heeled boots, red flared trousers, a green leather jacket, and a brown knitted hat.

Reports may be read by many who do not share the report writer's special knowledge.

PLACING PRONOUNS IN RIGHT RELATION TO ANTECEDENTS

Although it is best to avoid the use of "he" and "she" where proper names or identification tags (such as "Witness #1") can be used, there are instances in which the use of these pronouns is unavoidable. When this is the case, the police report writer must keep in mind the rule of English grammar which states that pronouns always refer back to the nearest antecedent.

Example—Suspect #2 was questioned by Officer Wilson. He said he had not been near the scene of the robbery that evening.

It is clear that the report writer meant to describe Suspect #2 saying that he wasn't near the scene of the robbery that evening. But that isn't what he has actually written. Instead, his sentence says that Officer Wilson wasn't near the scene of the robbery. The pronoun "he," beginning the second sentence, must refer back to the nearest antecedent—Officer Wilson.

Where people are interacting, the use of the pronouns "he" and "she" is likely to lead to confusion as to who the nearest antecedents are. If these pronouns are combined with labels, care must be taken to use the nearest antecedent rule.

Ineffective: R/O talked with Witnesses #1 and #2 at the
scene of the accident. He later questioned
Victim #2 at County Hospital.

Effective: Witnesses #1 and #2 were questioned by
R/O at the scene of the accident. He later
questioned Victim #2 at County Hospital.

The ineffective example has a misleading antecedent. The nearest
antecedent to the "he" beginning the second sentence is Witnesses #1
and #2. In the effective example, the antecedent of "he" is clearly the
R/O.

Avoiding Conclusions Based on Assumptions

Assumptions, as defined earlier, are statements which proceed from
opinions and beliefs of which we are unaware, and which we
therefore do not question. A police report must clearly relate the
statements it makes to their sources of verification. Describing people
who seem to be drunk is an example of a police report writing
situation in which assumptions may enter the report.

It is often tempting to describe seemingly intoxicated persons as
"drunks." However, without the results of a recognized test for
inebriation, such a description is a conclusion based on assumptions.

Ineffective: R/O noted that Suspect #2 was drunk at the
time he was questioned.

Effective: R/O noted that Suspect #2 was slur:ing his
speech, having trouble maintaining his
balance, smelled of what seemed to be
alcohol, and seemed to be drunk at the time
he was questioned.

or

Effective: Suspect #2's slurred speech, difficulty in
maintaining balance, and breath odor
suggested that he might have been drunk. A
blood test showed an alcohol level of 0.21%.

The writing here bridges a difficult gap in police procedure. On the one hand, the appearance of drunkenness may be significant to the consequences of the police action reported. But on the other, the writer must not assume a physical condition to exist without some objective proof.

This same problem occurs when reports of witnesses and victims appear in the police report. The writer must take care to distinguish between data personally observed, and data reported second hand.

Ineffective: Suspects took a total of $192.80 from the two cash registers.

Effective: Victim #1 reported to R/O that suspects took a total of $192.80 from the two cash registers, based on a register check done approximately two hours earlier.

In the first example, the reporting officer would have to have been there, auditing the theft, in order to possess such exact knowledge. Only in the second example is it clear that the source of the information is the victim, and that it is based on a specific inquiry.

When including information of a specific nature, or describing conditions with definite labels, report writers must continually ask themselves, "How do I know this?" "Can I prove this?"

AVOIDING INADVERTENT SUGGESTIONS OF IMPROPER PROCEDURE

Police reports are used by attorneys on both sides of a legal action. Defense attorneys often take a line of defense which is based on allegations that the police officers involved were guilty of improper, and therefore illegal, procedures. To support these allegations, the defense attorney may turn to evidence in the police report.

Police reports must be carefully written to include an account of all necessary procedures required for proper law enforcement. Omission of such procedural reporting, or ambiguity about the procedures used, leaves the way open for charges of improper conduct.

A good example of this procedural reporting is the Supreme Court decision known as the "Miranda Decision." This decision requires that persons be instructed of their rights at the time they are arrested.

The police report must include the information that such instruction was given if the reporting officers are to avoid charges of improper conduct. Some police departments have created a "neologism" (a new, or coined, word) of this process. Thus, a police report may include the expression "Mirandaed," "Mirandized," or "as per Miranda."

Ineffective: Suspect was apprehended leaving the scene of the robbery, and arrested.

Effective: Suspect was apprehended leaving the scene of the robbery, instructed of his rights per Miranda, and arrested.

In all other instances, where a police action is reported, those legal requirements for the performance of the action must be included in the report in order to present proper police procedure as it was actually practiced.

EDITING THE POLICE REPORT

Careful attention to the problems which have been discussed in this section is one way to avoid ambiguity in police report writing. ("Ambiguous" writing is unclear, indefinite, uncertain, vague.) Another way to avoid ambiguity is to acquire experience in editing police reports. This section includes a badly done police report to be edited. Follow the errors in the example report, and relate them back to the specific sections where such errors are discussed. This is a way to begin to acquire experience in editing police reports.

It is doubtful that anyone would be likely to make all these errors in one report. However, looking for all the errors, and discussing them, will focus attention on the kinds of errors that are most likely to creep into reports.

Example—Police Report

R/O's responded to a family beef call on Elmhurst Avenue at about 0300 hrs. We encountered a man who answered the door who said his wife, Mrs. Celia Johnston, had placed the call. Mr. Johnston was drunk and obnoxious. He said that dummy calls the cops everytime I say boo to her. R/O's requested Mr. Johnston's permission to enter the house; he assented. Inside, we found Mrs. Johnston sprawled around, also drunk. She was hard to understand but said that her husband had beat her up and threatened her with a weapon. R/O's found some possible weapons in the room, but the gun was unloaded. We asked Mr. Johnston if there were bullets for the gun in his house, whereupon Mrs. Johnston said he kept them in a box on the top of his desk. Mr. Johnston made a threatening gesture to Mrs. Johnston and was about to hit her. He was restrained although he resisted. He was therefore handcuffed. At this time, Mrs. Emily Armstrong, Mrs. Johnston's mother, entered the room from the rear of the house. She said I've been hiding but I heard you policemen so I came out. She said they were arguing over a stolen car. She interrupted, "You shut up, Mama." She said I don't care anymore, I'm sick of this and that they were involved in a series of car thefts which had recently been the source of violent arguments. She said it was she, and not her daughter, who had telephoned the police department. He said I knew we should have gotten rid of her along time ago. She said you shut up, you souse, you got us into this in the first place, now you get us out. We had received earlier reports of suspicious cars at this residence, and had requested a licence check and follow-up unit before responding to the house. The other officers now came to the door to inform us that two of the cars parked on the Johnston's front lawn and driveway had been reported stolen. We zapped the Johnston's and Mrs. Armstrong, following the usual procedure. I think we caught them redhanded.

The following, sentence-by-sentence analysis discusses the errors, as well as some of the good points, that this report demonstrates.

R/O's responded to *a family beef call* on Elmhurst Avenue at about 0300 hrs.

The reference to "a family beef call" is police jargon. It should be replaced by either the police dispatcher code for this kind of call, or the penal code reference to the particular disturbance reported, or ordinary wording such as "a report of a violent argument."

The next error is the reference, "on Elmhurst Avenue." The writer should have included the exact address. In the same way, the reference to "at about 0300 hrs." should be either an exact time or a range of time during which the officers arrived.

> *We* encountered *a man* who answered the door *who said* his wife, Mrs. Celia Johnston, had placed the call.

This sentence begins with an error. "I" and "we" should be avoided at all times. The reference should be to "R/O's" or some similar third person designation.

The reference to "a man" should be replaced by Mr. Johnston's full name. The expression, "who said," when followed by a summary of a statement, can be misconstrued as an indirect quotation instead of a summary. It is therefore best to consistently use the expression "who said that." (Note that commas would help after "man" and after "door.")

> Mr. Johnston was *drunk* and *obnoxious*.

This statement is a conclusion based on assumptions. No verification of Mr. Johnston's drunkenness is offered. The label "obnoxious" is not objective and cannot be supported under courtroom questioning. It is ambiguous, since it begs the question, "Relative to what?" It would have been better to give a specific description of Mr. Johnston's behavior, and then allow readers to draw their own conclusions.

> He *said that* dummy calls the cops *everytime* I say boo to *her*.

This is clearly a direct quotation. It should be written with a comma after "said," and then a set of quotation marks before "that" and after the period. Since these changes create a complete sentence within a sentence, the "t" in "that" should be capitalized. (Note that "every time" is two words, not one.)

> R/O's requested Mr. Johnston's permission to enter the house; he
> assented.

This is an instance of good police report writing. The writer includes proper police procedure so that no later claim of illegal entry can be made.

> Inside, we found Mrs. Johnston *sprawled around*, also *drunk.*

Again the writer is making an assumption about the condition of inebriation. Also, the expression "sprawled around" is ambiguous. The writer needs more specific words to describe Mrs. Johnston's behavior.

> She was hard to understand but said that her husband had *beat her up*
> and threatened her with *a weapon.*

"Beat her up" is not accurate language and should not be in the well written police report. On the other hand, these could be Mrs. Johnston's exact words describing what happened. If this is the case, leave these words but surround them with single quotation marks ('beat her up').

It is doubtful that Mrs. Johnston actually said, "He threatened me with a weapon." (Also, "a weapon" is too vague an expression; the writer should describe a specific weapon.) It would therefore be best, here too, for the writer to use Mrs. Johnston's exact words, surrounded by single quotation marks (for example,...and threatened her with 'his gun.')

> R/O's found *some possible weapons* in the room, but *the gun* was
> unloaded.

"Some possible weapons" is vague; the writer could have listed the exact weapons found. This is clearly evident from the following reference to "the gun." The weapons should be listed and labeled so it is clear which gun is being described.

We asked Mr. Johnston if there were bullets for the gun in
his house, whereupon Mrs. Johnston *said he* kept them in a
box on the top of his desk.

The "we" reference which begins the sentence should be changed to a
third person designation. The "said" phrase should be changed to
"said that." Otherwise, the "he" must refer back to Mrs. Johnston,
which is not the case.

> Mr. Johnston made a threatening gesture to Mrs. Johnston and *was*
> *about to hit her.* He was restrained although he resisted. He was
> therefore handcuffed.

This passage includes a conclusion of the writer's. It cannot be
proven that Mr. Johnston was about to hit Mrs. Johnston unless he
actually did so. This could be corrected by using the phrase "as
though he were going to." The rest of the passage is good police report
writing, because it outlines proper procedures taken.

> At this time, Mrs. Emily Armstrong, Mrs. Johnston's mother, entered the
> room from the rear of the house. *She said* I've been hiding but I heard you
> policemen so I came out. *She said* they were arguing over a stolen car.
> *She* interrupted, "You shut up, Mama."

From this point on, the report falls apart because the writer strings
together a series of misleading pronouns, and because the writer
mishandles the quotation format. The first "she said," regarding her
hiding, is a direct quotation, and should be surrounded with
quotation marks. The "she" refers back to Mrs. Armstrong, but,
considering the problems which lie ahead, it would probably have
been better to name her.

The second "she said," regarding the stolen car, is an indirect
quotation, and should begin with "she said *that.*" "She interrupted" is
where the trouble really begins. Grammatically, this must still be
Mrs. Armstrong talking—but we know, from the context, and from
the reference to "Mama," that it is really Mrs. Johnston speaking. She
should be named, "Mrs. Johnston," rather than being referred to as
"she."

She said *I* don't care anymore, I'm sick of this *and that they* were involved in a series of car thefts which had recently been the source of violent arguments. *She* said it was she, and not her daughter, who had telephoned the police department. *He said I* knew we should have gotten rid of her a long time ago. *She said* you shut up, you souse, you got us into this in the first place, now you get us *out.*

Here we have an example of just how badly confused a report can become when the pronouns and quoted material are improperly handled. The first sentence excerpted above should really be two sentences. In the first one, Mrs. Armstrong, clearly identified, says, in what should be correct direct quotation form, that she is sick of this matter and doesn't care what happens any more. The second sentence is the writer's summary of Mrs. Armstrong's revelations regarding the car thefts. Referring to "she," in the next sentence, as "Mrs. Armstrong" makes it clearer who placed the report call. "He" in the next sentence should be "Mr. Johnston," and his remarks should be in proper direct quotation format. (Note that "a long" is incorrectly written as one word having a different meaning, "along.")

The next sentence brings Mrs. Johnston back into the argument, although this would be hard to discern from the report. Her comments should also go in direct quotation format.

We had received *earlier reports* of suspicious cars at this residence, and *had requested* a *licence* check and follow-up unit before responding to house.

The "we" beginning this sentence is incorrect. It implies the reporting officers, but is probably a reference to "this department." (Note that "license" is misspelled.)

The account of the earlier reports, and of the follow-up request, belong at the beginning of this report. This is an example of material which is out of chronological order. The implications of the report would be clearer if this material were included at the beginning.

The other officers now came to the door to inform us that two of the cars parked on the Johnston's front lawn and driveway had been reported stolen.

"The other officers" introduced here should be named or labelled, even if their names and/or designations appear elsewhere on the report form.

> We *zapped* the Johnstons' and Mrs. Armstrong, *following the usual procedure.*

"Zapped" is vague jargon, and should be replaced with an account of the actual arrest and the charge made at the time. "Following the usual procedure" is also too vague. It leaves openings for accusations of improper procedure. The exact procedure followed should be reported.

> *I think we caught them redhanded.*

This sentence should be omitted. It is clearly the writer's conclusion, and has no place in a well written police report.

REVISING THE POLICE REPORT

This section presents a rewritten version of the police report we have been discussing. The revisions are based on the analysis above.

This is not, of course, a perfect report. There is no such thing. Each department has its own particular standards and procedures which report writers must follow. However, this report does utilize good communications skills. It is written in clear language and therefore easy to follow; it is not confusing.

Example—Revised Police Report

R/O's responded to a 418 at 3250 Elmhurst Ave. at 0310 hrs. This department had received earlier reports of suspicious cars at this address. A license check and follow-up unit were requested before responding. Upon arrival, R/O's encountered Mr. Frank Johnston, who answered the door and said that his wife, Mrs. Celia Johnston, had placed the call. Mr. Johnston was loud, confused, and smelled of alcohol. He said, "That dummy calls the cops every time I say boo to her." R/O's requested Mr. Johnston's permission to enter the house; he assented. Inside, R/O's encountered Mrs. Johnston, lying on a couch. She seemed drowsy and disoriented. The room smelled of alcohol. Mrs. Johnston was hard to understand at first because of her slurred speech. She did make it clear, however, that her husband had 'beat her up' and threatened her with 'his gun.' R/O's observed a knife, a club, and a gun lying about the room. On inspection, the gun proved to be unloaded. R/O's asked Mr. Johnston if he kept ammunition for the gun in his house. Mrs. Johnston said that he kept bullets in a box on the top of his desk. Mr. Johnston made a threatening gesture with his fists, as though he were about to hit Mrs. Johnston. He was restrained, although he resisted. He was therefore handcuffed. At this time, Mrs. Emily Armstrong, who identified herself as Mrs. Johnston's mother, entered the room from the rear of the house. She said, "I've been hiding, but I heard you policemen, so I came out." Mrs. Armstrong said that the Johnstons were arguing about a stolen car. Mrs. Johnston interrupted, "You shut up, Mama." Mrs. Armstrong replied, "I don't care any more, I'm sick of this." Mrs. Armstrong said that the Johnstons had been involved in a series of car thefts, which had recently been the source of violent arguments. Mrs. Armstrong further said that it was she, and not her daughter, who had telephoned the police department. Mr. Johnston said, "I knew we should have gotten rid of her a long time ago." Mrs. Johnston said, "Shut up, you souse, you got us into this in the first place, now you get us out." At this time, Officers Jones and Malik responded to the house as per the follow-up request. They reported that two of the cars parked on the Johnstons' front lawn and driveway had been reported stolen. The Johnstons were arrested on a PC215 and informed of their rights as per Miranda. Mrs. Armstrong was taken into custody as an accessory.

SUMMARY

Police academies teach uniform standards of police report writing; individual departments have their own particular requirements for the police report. Communication skills, used in writing the police report, help create public documents which are useful, and which favorably represent the writer's organization.

This chapter has presented specific techniques for writing clear and accurate police reports. The following eleven point check list includes the major areas of effective writing techniques discussed.

1. Provide accurate labels for each of the persons, places and things mentioned in your report.

2. Use accurate time citations, providing a realistic time range where exact time is not known.

3. Try to keep your account of events within chronological order.

4. Don't use jargon.

5. Be careful to use appropriate quotation format.

6. Watch out for misleading pronouns.

7. Explain each occurrence within your report, no matter how obvious it may seem to you.

8. Remain in the third person, describing the actions of "reporting officer" rather than telling what "I" did.

9. Avoid all personal assumptions, and the unverified conclusions which proceed from them.

10. Describe rather than label; let readers draw their own conclusions.

11. Include careful accounting of all required and proper police procedures.

Discussion Questions

1. At the beginning of this chapter the police report is described as using the narrative writing strategy. What effect would the use of the other three writing strategies have on police report writing?

2. What advantages do you see in using the direct quotation? What disadvantages do you see? Make the same comparisons for the indirect quotation.

3. Think of the sequence of processes which span the time from the observation of a police incident to the writing of a report about it. Correlate these processes with the communication model.

Exercises

1. Find a newspaper article which covers a police incident. Write a police report describing the incident.

2. Read the report you have written (exercise 1) as though you were the different persons who might actually read such a report: superior officer; district attorney; defense attorney; suspect; victim; witness; journalist; social worker. How would each of these persons react to your report? What would they be looking for? What might be their criticisms?

3. Observe a dramatized police incident, acted out by members of your class. Write your own police report, and compare it with those written by other observers in the class. What discrepancies in data appear? What differing conclusions are suggested by different reports?

INDEX